URBAN INJUSTICE

URBAN INJUSTICE

HOW GHETTOS HAPPEN

DAVID HILFIKER, M.D.

with a foreword by
MARIAN WRIGHT EDELMAN

SEVEN STORIES PRESS
New York | Toronto | London | Sydney

SEVEN STORIES PRESS
140 Watts Street
New York, NY 10013
http://www.sevenstories.com

In Canada:
Hushion House, 36 Northline Road, Toronto, Ontario M4B 3E2

In the U.K.:
Turnaround Publisher Services Ltd., Unit 3, Olympia Trading Estate,
Coburg Road, Wood Green, London N22 6TZ

In Australia:
Tower Books, 2/17 Rodborough Road, Frenchs Forest NSW 2086

Library of Congress Cataloging-in-Publication Data

Hilfiker, David.
Urban injustice : How ghettos happen / David Hilfiker.—1st ed.
p. cm.
Includes bibliographical references.
ISBN 1-58322-465-3
1. Urban poor—United States. 2. African Americans—Economic
conditions. I. Title.

HV4045 .H55 2002
362.5'08996'07301732—dc21
2001007353

9 8 7 6 5 4 3 2 1

College professors may order examination copies
of Seven Stories Press titles for a free six-month trial period.
To order, visit www.sevenstories.com/textbook,
or fax on school letterhead to (212) 226-1411.

Book design by M. Astella Saw

Printed in the U.S.A.

Contents

Seventeen years ago, three-year-old Anthony and four-year-old Maurice died in Dade County, Florida. Their mother worked to support her family but her income was too low to pay for child care. Since she qualified for government help she was put on Florida's long waiting list for child care assistance, a list with 22,000 names. While waiting she relied on friends and relatives to care for the children. Some days those arrangements fell through and the boys were left alone while she went to work. On one such day, Maurice and Anthony climbed into the clothes dryer to look at a magazine in a seemingly cozy place, closed the door, and tumbled and burned to death. The *Miami Herald* wrote, "There are hundreds, maybe thousands more tragedies waiting to happen in Dade County alone, in every home where young children are left to fend for themselves. They're not latchkey kids, they're lockup kids, locked inside for the day by parents who can't afford day care, can't afford not to work and can't get government assistance. Anthony and Maurice might be alive today if affordable care had been available."

Years later, in another American city, Antonio was born to Maria, a young mother who was sent home with him the day he was born. Only she didn't have a home. She was a single parent with no extended family support. She loved her baby and within the limits of public assistance was able to find a small room to rent. When Antonio was about three months old, Maria called a health clinic to report her baby was sick. The nurse told Maria to bring him in. Maria said she didn't have transportation. The nurse asked for the baby's symptoms and, after hearing Antonio had suffered diarrhea for two days, concluded he had a flu virus and advised Maria to keep the baby hydrated. "Feed the baby liquids every hour; Pedialyte or apple juice is good." Maria went to her refrigerator. She didn't have Pedialyte or apple juice or even ice. But in her cupboard she did have tomato sauce, so she filled the baby's bottle with it and stayed up all night feeding him every hour on the hour. The sodium content of the tomato sauce accelerated the baby's dehydration and by morning his tiny body was lifeless.

Anthony, Maurice, and Antonio died from poverty in the wealthiest nation on earth. Should Anthony and Maurice have died because their mother could not afford child care when she had to go to work to support them? Did Antonio need to die because his mother lacked transportation, adequate access to health care, and food? These were three real children, each a sacred gift of God, and a member of our American and human family. We could have prevented their deaths and thousands of other child deaths like theirs; we still have the opportunity to alleviate the daily terrors and perils millions of other poor children and families face by making more just choices in our rich, powerful nation.

Our nation's current budget choices favor powerful corporate interests and the wealthiest taxpayers over poor children and families' urgent needs. The gap between rich and poor is at its largest recorded point in more than thirty years. While thousands of children, parents, and grandparents stand in unemployment and soup kitchen and homeless shelter lines waiting for food and a stable place to live all across America, lobbyists for powerful corporations and rich individuals and special interests line up inside Congress and the White House and state houses to get hundreds of billions of dollars in new tax breaks and government handouts.

Follow the money and you find out what we truly care about and stand for as a nation. Budgets represent moral and social choices, not just economic ones. They are a test of what we value as a people. Our budget priorities say we do not value our children and poor families. Poor children, families, and individuals cannot eat promises, be sheltered from the cold by photo-ops, or escape poverty through eloquent speeches about compassion with crumbs from America's table of plenty.

It is morally shameful that a child is born into poverty every forty-three seconds, and without health insurance every minute in our nation. Persistent and pervasive poverty and child neglect in our country are not acts of God. They are moral and political choices we make as Americans. We can change them. We have the money. We have the power. We have the know-how. We have the experience. We have the vision. And we have the moral and social responsibility. What we lack is the civic and spiritual engagement of enough citizens, and political, faith, and media leaders to pierce the profound lack of awareness about and indifference to preventable and solvable child and adult suffering. As we seek the spiritual and civic resolve we require, we are hindered by the poisonous politics of self-interest and greed; narrow ideological agendas that reflect the belief that government should help the rich and powerful most and the poor and powerless least; and the political hypocrisy of leaders at all levels of government and in all parties who leave millions of children and families behind while pretending to do otherwise. Anthony's, Maurice's, and Antonio's stories are just the tip of the iceberg of the child suffering that affects millions of children every day and will sink our ship of state and nation's soul if we do not change course.

In his fine book, Dr. David Hilfker describes many of the underlying causes of poverty in our nation, especially black urban poverty; explains why past efforts have not eliminated poverty; and shows why and how we can and must do better. For our children's and nation's sakes, we need to approach present and future efforts to end child and family poverty with a new level of moral and political commitment, and urgency and vision. Now is the time for all of us to raise our voices and stand together to help America truly honor the ideals of freedom and justice for which it purports to stand. Like the widow in the New Testament parable who pestered the unjust judge, we need to speak up for justice again and again and again until our requests to leave no child or person behind in the richest nation on earth are heard and acted upon. America has been blessed with so much. Let us determine to be a blessing to all the poor in our own nation and around the world.

MARIAN WRIGHT EDELMAN
President, Children's Defense Fund

Introduction

When we Americans want to do something about poverty, we usually set about "improving" poor people. We may offer education or job training, establish programs to develop the parenting skills of young mothers, require addiction treatment as a condition for receiving housing, put a time limit on welfare benefits in order to motivate poor people to work, or refuse additional welfare payments to discourage further childbearing.

This practice of improving poor people has a long history. Early American reformers traced extreme poverty to intoxication, laziness, and other kinds of unacceptable behavior. They tried to use public policy and philanthropy to elevate poor people's characters and change their behavior. As the years passed, different sets of behaviors were blamed for poverty and successive methods suggested to improve the poor. Later reformers looked to evangelical religion, temperance legislation, punitive poor houses, the forced breakup of families, and threats of institutionalization—all to improve poor people.

This approach has rested on the persistent belief that the individual faults of the poor are the primary causes of poverty: ignorance, lack of training, addiction, laziness, defective character, sexual promiscuity, too many children; the list goes on and on. It is not surprising, of course, that a nation so strongly committed to individualism should so often search for the roots of poverty within the poor persons themselves.

In this short book, I want to consider poverty from a different vantage point. I want to suggest that the primary causes of poverty lie not in individual behavior at all, but in specific social and historical structures, in forces outside any single person's control. This is not to deny that most poor people's character could use some improving (as could most of the rest of ours), but it is to suggest that the essential causes of American poverty lie elsewhere: in the paucity of jobs on which someone might support a family, in inadequate access to health care and child care, in meager educational resources, in specific government policies, in nonexistent vocational training, in the workings of the criminal justice system, and, for African Americans, in a painful history of slavery, segregation, and discrimination.

The American stereotype of poverty has become the single-parent, black, inner-city family. And, indeed, African Americans are three times more likely to be poor than whites. In the 2000 Census,[1] however, almost half (46.8 percent) of America's poor were white, close to another quarter (23.0 percent) were Hispanic, and 6.2 percent were Native American, Asian, and Pacific Islander. Only just over one-quarter (26.2 percent) were African Americans. Of those poor Americans, almost a quarter (22.0 percent) lived in rural areas and more than a third (36.4 percent) in suburbs. Of African Americans in poverty, less than half live in the urban ghettos that have come to be the almost exclusive definition of poverty in the American mind.

This book is largely about those black Americans, only about 12 percent of all our poor people, who do live in the inner-city ghettos. Many other books could be (and have been) written about white poverty, about Hispanic poverty, about Native American poverty, about poverty in general. Why, then, is this white, middle-class physician writing about black, urban poverty?

The simplest answer is that it's what I know about.

In 1983, after seven years as a rural physician in northeastern Minnesota, I moved to Washington, D.C., to practice medicine in two small inner-city clinics. African Americans are Washington's predominant population and—aside from immigrant groups that have recently been expanding—the poor here are overwhelmingly black. For five years, my family and I lived in Christ House, a medical recovery shelter for homeless men. In 1990, we started Joseph's House, a community and hospice for formerly homeless men dying with AIDS, where we lived for three years. For almost two decades, then, I have lived and worked among the black, urban poor. Their plight has been my primary professional concern.

More important, what I know about and what concerns me the most unfortunately fits all too well with both public and media stereotypes of poverty. When most Americans think about poverty, or see the poor on television, or read about them in the newspapers, the images are of poor black men hanging around the street corner, poor black teenagers selling drugs, poor black single mothers living on welfare, poor black inner-city schools failing their children. In spite of the statistics, in our country poverty has become synonymous with black, urban poverty. Since the late 1960s, when President Lyndon B. Johnson's War on Poverty ended in "failure," poverty has been almost a code word for the inner-city black ghetto, its drugs and its crime. If, then, we are going to face the larger questions of what to do about poverty in America, there's really no way to go but through the ghetto—both as it really exists and as most Americans imagine it.

Finally, I'm writing about poverty and the ghetto because the reasons for their existence and the links between them are not at all mysterious but lie clearly in history. It's nowhere near as hard as most of us imagine to grasp the causes of black, urban poverty (or, for that matter, white, rural poverty), and it's important not to attribute those causes simply to slavery. If we were to decide to put our minds, our energy, and some of our nation's resources to work, there are solutions we could choose. Right now.

Yes, most of us tend to ascribe poverty to the behavior of the poor themselves, and yet, if we were honest, we would admit to at least some puzzlement over, say, why young black children are four times more likely to be poor than their white counterparts, or even why the black ghetto exists in the first place.

I am no stranger to the individual weaknesses of the poor and black in America. It's the nature of a doctor's work to see people who are in trouble one at a time, and it has often seemed to me that the immediate causes of my patients' poverty *did* lie in their own behavior. For some, addictions consumed their time and energy. Others would not (or could not) cooperate with my medical treatment plans. Still others lacked parenting skills or discernible job skills. Or all of the above. And some just didn't seem to want to work.

But the more time I spent with even the most troubled of my patients, the more obvious it became that virtually all of them were doing close enough to the best they could in the overwhelmingly difficult environment they inhabited. The odds against which they struggle, however, are massive. If you haven't lived it or even seen it firsthand, there's almost no way to imagine it. Living in the ghetto, one faces problems with public housing, family violence, drug and alcohol abuse, the drug trade, negligent landlords, criminals, illness, guns, isolation, hunger, ethnic antagonisms, racism, and other obviously negative forces. Even forces that might seem positive in other circumstances—the law, the media, government, neighbors, police—can, in the ghetto context, make life miserable for the poor. And one has to contend with all of these forces—any one of which might be overwhelming—all at once, without a break. Turn to deal with one problem, and three attack you from behind. Experience a little unexpected bad luck, and you find yourself instantly drowning. The cumulative effect of the "surround"[2] is more than the sum of any of these individual forces. There is simply no space to breathe.

When I first arrived in Washington, I was already familiar with many of the structural causes of poverty. But like so many of us, I was convinced that if the individual could be strengthened enough, he or she could make it out of the ghetto, and if enough people could be strengthened, the ghetto itself would collapse. I have spent the better part of a professional career trying to strengthen individual poor people. While that may have been a positive endeavor, I no longer believe that individual efforts to improve individual poor people will substantially reduce poverty.

The argument that inner-city poverty comes primarily from the personal weaknesses of poor people simply cannot be sustained. Among African-American children under the age of six, *half* live in poverty. Among African-American males between the ages of eighteen and thirty-four in the city of Washington, *half* are in the criminal justice system.[3] There are only two possible explanations for these and many similar statistics. Either African Americans are genetically predisposed to poverty, or specific forces in their environment have kept large numbers poor!

For centuries, whites have consciously or unconsciously found the explanation in theories of racial inferiority.[4]

In this book, I will argue what has long been evident to African Americans and should long since have been obvious to everyone else: something awful has been done to the black poor in this country. Allowing for that monumental injustice, however, how does one explain the individual behavioral deficiencies that seem so prevalent among poor African Americans (and other groups of Americans in poverty)? How can one account for the extraordinarily high rates of single parenthood, widespread substance abuse, problematic parenting, and criminal behavior within the black ghettos? If the reason is not some genetic inferiority, what does cause these problems in the first place? And why do they persist?

Even after a decade of practicing medicine in the inner city, I found I couldn't answer those questions in ways that satisfied me. This proved so frustrating that, in a foolhardy moment, I volunteered to teach a course on the causes of urban poverty. It was undoubtedly my way of putting myself on a collision course with what I felt I still needed to learn. In search of answers, I plunged into an extensive, often impressive, and remarkably consistent library of books and articles of all sorts on the nature, causes, and consequences of urban poverty. I was often shocked at how little I had known.[5]

The result is this book, for which I make no claim to originality. Quite the opposite. What I've tried to do is take the work of many scholars and journalists—often long, sometimes inspiring, but also sometimes dry or written for academic peers—and condense the essence into a single, short work that might explain urban poverty to anyone: exactly the book that in all those rushed years of doctoring I might have longed for and used.

Complex as urban poverty and the behaviors that surround it might seem, there is, in fact, a certain basic simplicity to the problem and to the sorts of solutions that are (this perhaps surprised me more than anything) not hopelessly utopian and suitable only for an unimaginable, distant future. These solutions are, instead, remarkably close at hand, practical, and capable of being instituted were we only of a political mind to do so.

After a decade of unprecedented economic prosperity in the richest country the world has ever known, the poverty rate at the time of the 2000 Census was at its lowest in a generation. Nevertheless, 11.3 percent of all Americans, more than one out of every nine people, lived below an official poverty level that severely underestimates what most of us would consider poverty. Even more distressing, almost one out of six American children under eighteen (16.2 percent[6]) and almost one out of three of African-American children under eighteen (30.9 percent[7]) lived in poverty. Why?

One

BUILDING THE GHETTO: A HISTORY

Racial segregation has been a characteristic of American society for almost four hundred years, but the movement toward residential segregation so familiar to us today began less than a century ago. Before 1910, urban African Americans were far more likely to have whites as neighbors than other blacks.[1] By the beginning of the 1950s, however, African-American urban neighborhoods were highly segregated, often physically isolated, densely concentrated, and fully formed. But these neighborhoods differed significantly from their modern counterparts. Though poorer on average than white neighborhoods, these black ghettos were, by and large, vibrant communities that "worked." They were societies unto themselves that mirrored the larger society.

How did such neighborhoods come to be and what happened to them to create the abysmal conditions we know as the "urban ghetto"?

BLUEPRINT FOR THE GHETTO

Though a black elite of freedmen who earned their living as artisans and professionals had already established itself in the industrial cities of the North before the Civil War, African Americans began moving north in modest numbers only in the decades following the abolition of slavery. Former slaves in the South had been given no land upon emancipation, and so were forced into a sharecropping system in which workers "rented" land from white landowners with large holdings, paying their rents out of the year's produce. While sharecropping was an improvement upon slavery, it still left the worker at the mercy of the landowner. Somehow, at the end of the year's reckoning, the sharecropper was still in debt. Persistently poor, former slaves found themselves unable to accumulate enough money to buy land for themselves. In addition, southern agriculture was distinctly seasonal, so there were long periods of idleness, often enforced by contracts with the landowners that prohibited other forms of remunerated work, even during the off-season. With the end of Reconstruction in 1877, African Americans also faced disenfranchisement, lynchings, legal segregation, and the first of a host of Jim Crow laws that ultimately left them with virtually none of the rights of citizenship.

Meanwhile, the industrialization of northern cities was in full swing, creating factory jobs at wages unheard of in the South. Initially, these jobs brought to the cities large numbers of immigrants, mostly European, mostly white. A trickle of largely uneducated African-American workers coming north could still find work, but they faced considerable discrimination in the cities, especially in employment. Their wages were lower than whites', their chances for advancement were poor, and they were rarely allowed to join unions. Nevertheless, pressures in the South pushed and possibilities in the North pulled small numbers of African Americans into northern cities—only about 400,000 between the end of the Civil War and the outbreak of World War I. In 1910, African Americans were no more than 5 percent of the population of any northern industrial city.

The influx of millions of European immigrants in the late 1800s created a patchwork of different ethnic communities in those cities. Since public transportation was virtually nonexistent and most new immigrants could not afford to move away from the places where they worked, the different ethnic enclaves where culture and language were familiar tended to cluster around the factories and sweatshops. Black "immigrants" from the South followed the same pattern.

These early immigrant clusters differed from ghettos[2] in several respects. First, they were never homogeneous: many different nationalities coexisted in the same neighborhoods. Second, as factory workers became more affluent, they or their children moved out of the ghetto and dispersed into the general population. Third, as a result of this dispersion, a majority of any ethnic group almost always lived outside of identifiable clusters. Thus, while new immigrants continued to move into ethnic enclaves, families who had been there longer tended to disperse throughout the city.

By the early 1900s, however, the character of the African-American clusters in the North began to change. Blacks faced increasing discrimination in housing and public accommodations. Resistance to integration hardened, so it became more difficult to move out of the black enclaves. Continuing union opposition to black members and employer reluctance to train them as skilled workers in the factories kept African Americans in jobs that were "heavy, hot, dirty and low-paying."[3] The northern white press increasingly joined its Southern counterparts in portraying African Americans in stereotypical terms and as inferior to whites. Segregation became more pronounced. By 1910, despite the low numbers of blacks in northern cities and despite the fact that the average African American in those cities still lived in a ward that was less than 10 percent black, the outlines of the future black ghetto were beginning to emerge.

What came to be called "The Great Migration" of African Americans from the rural South began with the outbreak of World War I and a spike in the need for factory workers in the North. Although the United States did not join the war until 1917, American factories sold supplies to the Allied combatants from the beginning. Industry found a source of cheap labor in southern blacks and actively recruited them. Under the impact of the war and in the 1920s, between 1.5 and 2 million largely unskilled African Americans moved north; an additional 400,000 followed during the 1930s.

The Depression, of course, meant poverty for many people, but African-American workers, at the bottom of the pecking order, were the first to be let go and the hardest hit. As the economy gradually picked up during the later thirties, white workers were the first rehired, leaving disproportionate numbers of African Americans on relief or in federal work camps. To make matters worse, African Americans were largely excluded from the most important of President Franklin D. Roosevelt's New Deal programs to alleviate poverty. Social Security and mandatory unemployment insurance, for example, were two of the central elements of social insurance introduced during the Depression, but they both specifically excluded domestics and agricultural workers. Since two-thirds of employed African Americans were then either domestics or agricultural workers, most blacks were not eligible for benefits. While the rest of the country was receiving significant Federal help moving out of poverty, African Americans were generally left out.

The Federal Housing Administration (FHA), another important anti-poverty agency established during the Depression, guaranteed mortgages for up to 90 percent of the purchase price of a house, making down payments of 10 percent the norm, and it also extended the repayment period to twenty-five or thirty years. Previously, lenders had required down payments of up to one-third the cost of a home's purchase price, making home ownership impossible for many. During the waning years of the Depression and again after World War II, FHA guarantees not only allowed families to become homeowners (and thus accumulate wealth), but also created local jobs and provided investment in the community. Between 1934, when the FHA was founded, and 1969, the percentage of families owning their own homes increased from 44 percent to 64 percent. Citing concerns that poorer black neighborhoods were not good financial risks, however, the FHA "redlined" almost all African-American communities, refusing to guarantee mortgages there. Private lenders followed suit. After World War II, the Veterans Administration used the same redlining policies, ensuring that returning African-American servicemen were excluded from the program. These policies excluding African Americans from government largesse lasted well into the 1960s.

Between 1940 and 1960, a staggering 4.5 million blacks left the South, a second Great Migration to northern cities. Because of segregation, however, the geographic area of the already established black ghettos in these cities expanded only slowly, leaving these new immigrants few options for housing. In addition, cities were increasingly turning to zoning in an effort to separate residential from industrial areas. When zoning choices had to be made among neighborhoods, the politically less powerful black communities were usually the losers, tending to be zoned as "industrial," a label that often prohibited not only the construction of new residential construction but even the improvement of old residential buildings. The quality of life in these areas was already lower because of neighboring industry, and what housing stock existed tended to deteriorate easily. Non-blacks, of course, were free to look elsewhere and move out of their impoverished neighborhoods into better housing, but the realities of segregation forced African Americans to remain in these increasingly industrialized urban areas.

As a result, population density in the black ghetto increased steadily. By 1950, the average "isolation index" in northern ghettos was almost 90 percent, meaning that, on average, African Americans lived in neighborhoods that were 90 percent black, a level of segregation never experienced by any European ethnic group in the United States.

IMPOVERISHING THE GHETTO

Despite the crowding, northern black ghettos in 1950 were viable communities. Poverty created its share of social problems (the average income of African-American families then was only slightly more than half that of white families), and these neighborhoods were segregated racially, but, in spite of some degree of class separation within the black ghetto, neighborhoods were largely "vertically integrated." Affluent, middle-class, working-class, and poor people all lived in relatively close proximity. Social organization was intact. Informal networks kept neighbors in touch with one another, while businesses, schools, churches, fraternal organizations, and volunteer organizations supported viable communities. Most people held jobs. Single-parent families were a distinct minority. Levels of violence were low. Education was valued.

To offer a personal example, my father directed a settlement house in the ghetto of St. Louis, Missouri, from 1946 to 1950. He tells of searching frequently for kids in trouble and—as a white man—having to run up and down the dark staircases of urban tenements late at night. He remembers no feelings of fear. There wasn't, he says, anything to be afraid of.

A series of events over the next three decades, however, changed this situation radically, creating the modern black ghetto. The first of these events was the wholesale destruction of black neighborhoods by the federal Urban Renewal and the federal Interstate Highway programs. Urban renewal (then called "slum removal") was initially meant to revive decaying inner-city neighborhoods by transforming them into new, architecturally interesting cultural, commercial, and residential centers. Again, because African Americans generally held less political power, black ghettos were often the chosen sites for slum removal. Significant parts of black ghettos were razed and rebuilt, often as magnets for business or tourism, such as the Loop in Chicago, the Gateway Arch in St. Louis, or (somewhat later) the Inner Harbor in Baltimore. Not without justice were the slum renewal programs sometimes called "Negro removal."

As part of urban renewal, the federal government provided money for the construction of some new public housing for those displaced by the changes. Reasoning that limited resources should go to the poor, Congress set strict income limits on who could live in these new housing "projects." Functionally, this meant that the poorest members of the black ghetto were moved somewhere else in the city and segregated by class as well as by race, only intensifying their isolation from the larger society. The worst of these projects were high-rise towers that housed many people in small geographic areas. In addition, such public housing provided on average only one unit for every ten units destroyed. The rest of those evicted by urban renewal had to squeeze into whatever already overcrowded ghetto areas remained. One Chicago critic pointed out that since local residents "were already living in coal-bins, out-houses, and other cubbyholes of squalor,"[4] there were few places left to squeeze into.

The Interstate Highway program instituted in 1956 by President Dwight D. Eisenhower repeated the process. As a network of superhighways meant to link the country together was blasted through cities, poor black areas were, not surprisingly, the first choices for disruption. Either an area would be razed and its former inhabitants removed, or a highway would be placed so as to create a physical boundary between the black ghetto and other areas of the city, further isolating its inhabitants.

The federally subsidized highway programs also facilitated the suburbanization of the North, contributing to the erosion of its cities. Increasingly affluent whites were eager to leave those cities, and the government subsidized this exodus by building roads that made daily access to urban workplaces from the suburbs far more feasible. FHA and Veterans Administration mortgage guarantees, more easily given for new housing in new neighborhoods and completely unavailable for black or mixed urban neighborhoods, encouraged (white) families with even modest incomes to invest in suburban home ownership. Between 1950 and 1970, seven million whites left center cities.[5]

The effects of this "white flight" were drastic, not only concentrating the population of poor African Americans in center cities, but also drawing jobs away from those same areas, especially jobs that paid a living wage.

By the middle of the twentieth century, the United States had become the overwhelming leader in worldwide manufacturing.

Many of its factories were still located in the large cities of the North. They offered good employment, even for workers who entered the job market with little education and few skills. By this time, most unions accepted African Americans—there were also primarily black unions—and high levels of unionization in industry meant that jobs were secure, wages relatively high, and chances for advancement good if one stayed with the company. During the immediate post–World War II period, such blue-collar jobs were the primary way out of poverty for many African Americans.

Major structural changes in the global economy over the last four decades, however, have drastically altered that situation. After the destruction caused by World War II, the Europeans and Japanese gradually rebuilt their manufacturing sectors, which by the 1970s had begun to compete, often quite successfully, with American companies. In the later 1980s and 1990s, less developed countries like Korea and Taiwan expanded their manufacturing, too. By the turn of the millennium, American manufacturing was competing not only with the Chinese manufacturing juggernaut but also the former Eastern Bloc nations, Mexico, and Latin America.

Within the United States, changes in technology and transportation eliminated the need to locate factories in the middle of cities, so industry, too, joined the exodus to the suburbs. Rural areas in the North and the cities and suburbs in the Sun Belt of the Southwest also proved increasingly attractive to industry because land was cheaper, taxes lower, and unions far weaker. More recently, the development of large, transnational corporations able to create "global assembly lines" has led to further loss of manufacturing in the United States as "American" plants move to the Third World, where wages are drastically lower, unions often nonexistent, environmental laws few, and expensive regulations to protect workers from harm seldom on the books, much less enforced.

With the increasing computerization and mechanization of manufacturing worldwide, moreover, many of the better-paying jobs that remain in the United States require higher levels of education. There are jobs for those who analyze data, write computer programs, manage people, administer organizations, or do financial planning. Increasingly, however, the bulk of jobs remaining for poorly trained or educated people are in the service sector—as domestics, janitors, clerks, salespeople, nursing aides, or cashiers—where wages have historically been low and benefits poor or nonexistent. To make matters worse, over the last thirty years, wages in the service sector have declined both in real dollars and relative to other sectors of the economy, so even full-time workers in such jobs now find it difficult to stay out of poverty.

A continuing pattern of residential segregation that is no less rigid for being informal makes it that much more difficult to find well-paying jobs outside of black areas. Yes, poor African Americans can get jobs in the suburbs, but only the most persistent succeed. Not only is discrimination in employment still a problem, but public transportation from the center city to the suburbs is also complicated, unreliable, and, most of all, time-consuming. Owning a car is too expensive for low-wage earners, especially for young men who must pay soaring urban insurance premiums.

Paradoxically, the success of the Civil Rights movement in bringing the end of legal segregation contributed to the devastation of the inner cities. African Americans could for the first time demand housing outside the crowded ghetto. So, beginning in the late 1950s, more affluent African Americans joined the white exodus from the city to the suburbs.[6] Only those who could not afford to move out were left.

The end result of all these changes is the black urban ghetto we know today. As early as the 1970s, what had been poor but vertically integrated neighborhoods had largely been transformed into poverty-stricken, resource-destitute areas where *only* poor people lived, lacking social networks, institutions of support, or jobs.

In most cases, as more affluent African Americans departed, these ghettos became physical wastelands, too. Business followed the money, leaving behind only a few corner grocery stores, occasional check-cashing places, liquor stores, and lots of boarded up buildings. The "surround of force" that people experienced led to despair, inertia, and increasing anti-social behavior.

The black ghetto had been plundered.

THE MYTH OF THE WAR ON POVERTY

For the majority of Americans, poverty had been a phenomenon of the Great Depression that essentially disappeared from the political radar screen with the economic stimulus of World War II and the consumerism of the post-war years. The 1950s were a time, it seemed, of economic prosperity; a time to move to the suburbs, start a family, and concentrate on one's own standard of living. Rock-and-roll music emerged, echoing the times: bold, impudent, full of hope and energy. The election of the young John F. Kennedy as president in 1960 symbolized the hopefulness with which the country looked toward the future.

There were rumblings, of course. The 1954 Supreme Court *Brown v. Board of Education* decision and the 1956 Montgomery, Alabama, bus boycott marked the beginning of the Civil Rights movement, which over the next fifteen years turned a spotlight on some of the poorest and most racist parts of the country. Northern whites began to develop a consciousness of segregation and also, to some degree, the poverty it engendered.

In 1962, political activist Michael Harrington published *The Other America*, a book that pointed to "invisible" poverty in the United States, to an economic underworld comprising nearly one-fifth of the population. Harrington focused graphically on the poverty of white rural areas such as the Appalachian hills, but looked at other groups, too: the uninsured elderly, migrant farm workers—and residents of the black ghettos. The book was published at a propitious moment. It not only symbolized a renewed curiosity about and urge to solve America's domestic problems, but also became itself part of the political process. The United States had won World War II, infused new life through the Marshall Plan into the devastated countries of Europe, and was both admired and feared throughout the world. Kennedy had announced that we would put a man on the moon before the end of the decade. Why, then, couldn't we solve poverty and civil rights—both problems located, for most Americans, far away in the backward South, primitive Appalachia, or the ignored inner-city ghettos? We were, after all, a "can-do" country.

In 1964, during his first months in office after the assassination of President Kennedy, President Lyndon B. Johnson felt the need for a grand theme to characterize his presidency, a program that would both offer him legitimacy in a position he had only inherited and garner the support of the liberals who had backed Kennedy and mistrusted this prototypical southern politician. Influenced by Harrington's book, Johnson declared a "war on poverty" as part of an ambitious attempt to complete the social revolution of the New Deal. Under the rubric of The Great Society, he launched a series of programs that significantly increased public spending on poverty, expanding services for and raising benefits available to the poor, especially to the elderly poor.

Johnson intended to focus the War on Poverty on white rural poverty, but as the Civil Rights movement gathered steam and the nation became increasingly aware of inner-city poverty, the spotlight shifted to the ghetto. Unfortunately, his War on Poverty was soon cut off at the knees by several converging factors, the most important of which was the war in Vietnam. As the war heated up in the mid-1960s, Johnson's energies focused increasingly on Vietnam, while political disagreements about the conduct of the war divided the liberal coalition that supported the reforms of his domestic agenda. Most decisive, money funneled to Vietnam could not be used to fight American poverty. Few of Johnson's poverty programs were ever fully implemented, and funding, never abundant, was curtailed or eliminated for almost all of them.

As our involvement in Vietnam withdrew resources from the war on poverty, the struggle for civil rights moved into northern cities and splintered. To white supporters of integration, the most threatening of the pieces was the Black Power movement. Previously strong supporters of civil rights in the South, northern liberal whites now felt themselves attacked by their former allies. The undertones of violence in Black Power were intimidating. Civil rights, a distant issue that to northern whites had seemed so easy to deal with, had suddenly shown up right in their backyard, morally ambiguous, and amenable to no simple solutions. Whereas 68 percent of northern whites supported Johnson's initiatives in 1964, just two years later 52 percent thought the government was pushing integration too fast.[7] Although the War on

Poverty was distinct from the Civil Rights movement, the two began to merge in public perception. As support drained for the latter, it was withdrawn from the former as well.

It was precisely then that the ghettos erupted in violence. The concentration of poverty and the isolation of the poor within American cities now created overwhelming pressures and frustrations amid all the promises of help and hope. Beginning in the Watts neighborhood of Los Angeles in 1965, one city after another boiled over. Television pictures of National Guardsmen occupying the smoldering ruins of the inner city would by 1968 become a dominant image of the black ghetto. Suddenly, poverty was not white, rural, and hardworking—"the great-, great-, grandchildren of Daniel Boone"[8]—but black, urban, and violent. Media images of the dangerous ghetto were now everywhere.

In 1964, Daniel Patrick Moynihan, then a young advisor to President Johnson, wrote what was supposed to be a confidential memo to the president. Although the report, *The Negro Family: The Case for National Action*, stressed male unemployment as the primary cause of black poverty, Moynihan also described what he called a "tangle of pathology" that had undermined the black family, another way of describing what Harrington (and others) had more positively, if blandly, called a "culture of poverty." While both Harrington and Moynihan wrote hoping to spur the country to action, in fact, the public began to interpret that "tangle of pathology" as an intractable and intrinsic feature of black urban life. Although Moynihan believed that more and better jobs for black men were a crucial part of the solution to poverty in the inner cities, he left that recommendation out of the final report, reinforcing a sense of the intractability of poverty. There were, it seemed, no solutions.

The Moynihan Report was leaked to the public just prior to the violence in Watts and then sensationalized in the press. It caused a firestorm among liberals and black activists, who interpreted it as humiliating to African Americans at a time when they were trying to support black strength and identity. Radical Black Power advocates condemned the report as another racist attempt to discredit black people and blame them for their plight. What right did this white man have even to write such a report about black people?

To exacerbate negative public perceptions, by the end of the decade the War on Poverty had actually succeeded in signing up nine out of ten eligible single mothers for the Aid to Families with Dependent Children (AFDC) program that Roosevelt had initiated thirty years earlier. Instead of small numbers of widows and their children receiving assistance, the welfare rolls were flooded with divorced and never-married mothers. Although it continued to serve more white than black families, during the 1960s the program came to be associated in the media (and therefore in the public mind) with young, black, urban single mothers. The black ghetto had become very visible—and very threatening.

Johnson came to office in the fall of 1963. The first of the Great Society programs moved through Congress and into rapid implementation in 1964. But the ghettos began exploding in 1965, and Vietnam was heavily draining the nation's financial resources by late 1966. The War on Poverty ground to a halt before it had begun to take off. According to historian Michael Katz, in the end the Office of Economic Opportunity (the hub of the War on Poverty) received less than 10 percent of the most conservative estimate of what it needed to reach its goals, spending about $70 per poor person per year. It never reached the takeoff point normal in most federal programs.

In reality, then, the War on Poverty proved to be only the briefest of skirmishes. The country gave itself no real chance to do anything about poverty. Of course, it wasn't coincidental that once poverty was defined as an African-American phenomenon, we gave up remarkably quickly.

Worse yet, the perceived failure of the Great Society programs now became associated with a hopelessly flawed "big government" approach to poverty that, in "throwing money" at problems, was believed to worsen them. The shadow of the aborted War on Poverty thus continues to hang over the discussion of poverty and its solutions. It is more than ironic—as well as further evidence of our deep-seated attitudes—that this tiny window of underfunded action that lasted barely a few years has become *prima facie* evidence of the government's inability ever to do anything about poverty—as if we had ever *tried* throwing money at poverty, much less committed ourselves to a program that might stand some chance of working.

Within a few short years we had gone from Harrington's *The Other America*, identifying a "culture of poverty" passed down from generation to generation and calling us to action, to the Moynihan Report, identifying a "tangle of pathology," almost a call to *in*action. What, after all, can be done about a "pathology"? Within a few short years, before we had really tried anything substantive, ghetto poverty had become, we believed, intractable.

Two

PILLAGING THE GHETTO:
OTHER CAUSES OF POVERTY

The causes of poverty are always multiple, interrelated, and mutually reinforcing. Examining some of the forces that have shaped the black ghetto, we must remember that separate descriptions of individual issues cannot adequately convey their combined impact, for each affects the other, increases the complexity, multiplies the difficulty, pulls the web tighter, adds to the surround of force. It is the complex sum of all these forces that is so discouraging.

"I'M NOT PREJUDICED, BUT..."

Discrimination based on skin color is still widespread in the United States. While there has undoubtedly been progress in the last half-century, discrimination against African Americans and other people of color remains a powerful strand in the web that traps ghetto residents in poverty.

Until relatively recently in our history, there has been little systematic effort to treat African Americans equally, and the intensity of the endless history of discrimination was a major factor in creating the ghetto environment. *Past* racial discrimination is still powerfully embedded in *current* social, political, and physical structures, and thus remains a potent cause of contemporary inner-city poverty.

Discrimination itself persists, of course, most notably, in housing and employment. In study after study, when paired couples similar to one another in every respect except color are sent out to purchase homes or rent housing, white couples will be shown housing that black couples were told was unavailable and black couples will be steered to black neighborhoods. It still remains difficult for African Americans—especially those living in ghetto areas—to obtain mortgage loans.

Studies of hiring practices show similar patterns. William Julius Wilson's in-depth examination of employer attitudes in Chicago demonstrates clearly that they are reluctant to hire young, black men from the inner city, although they perceive black women less negatively.[1] It is hard to determine, however, whether this attitude results more from racial bias or from a form of "geographic profiling," the tendency to exclude inner-city residents based on the belief that the ghetto is unlikely to produce acceptable employees. This point was underscored in Wilson's study by the fact that black employers judged this group of men just as harshly as did white employers, viewing them not only as uneducated, but also as unstable, uncooperative, and inherently dishonest.

Deliberately or not, employers screen out black, inner-city applicants. They may refuse to consider otherwise adequately qualified applicants simply because they went to urban public schools, or they may avoid taking referrals from welfare programs or state employment services. On the theory that friends of good workers are more likely to be reliable than applicants pulled from the general population, employers often look to recommendations from their current employees when hiring for less-skilled positions. This means that job hunters living in areas of high poverty where few of their friends work face almost insuperable problems simply finding out about openings. In Chicago, Wilson found, most employers do not advertise in the classifieds. Those who do are more likely to use ethnic, neighborhood, or suburban newspapers than citywide editions.[2]

The dialect of the black ghetto, black English vernacular, can also lead to problems. The ability to speak, write, and communicate effectively in standard English is essential for employment in most white-collar jobs (meaning that most ghetto residents will be considered only for blue-collar work). But even blue-collar employers frequently make use of language as a screening device. While black English vernacular has, in fact, all the rules and grammar of any dialect, white employers in particular may interpret its use as a reflection of lack of intelligence or ability. If he does not speak standard English well, a prospective employee may fail the "telephone test," never even making it to an initial interview. While it may be easy enough to sympathize with an employer looking for qualified applicants, from the point of view of the job seeker, discrimination by geographic profiling is no less virulent than a straightforward prejudice against African Americans.

It is no longer acceptable in many white circles to admit to racial prejudice, but as recently as 1990, a National Opinion Research survey of non-black respondents found that 65 percent thought blacks were lazier than other groups; 56 percent thought them more prone to violence; 53 percent saw them as less intelligent; and 78 percent thought them less self-supporting and more likely to live off welfare.[3]

AMERICAN APARTHEID

The continuing severe segregation of African Americans from the rest of society is undoubtedly the single most important cause of urban black poverty.[4] The ghetto itself is the problem.

Although the degree of black segregation in the United States has declined somewhat in the last decade, African Americans in every large northern city are still more segregated than *any* European ethnic group has *ever* been in *any* American city.[5] Sociological analysis uses several different statistical indices of segregation. Perhaps the most common is the "index of dissimilarity," which calculates the percentage of a minority population that would have to move into other neighborhoods in order to achieve an even distribution. Imagine, for example, a city that is 20 percent black. An even distribution, therefore, would mean that each neighborhood was 20 percent black. The index of similarity is the percentage of the city's blacks who would have to move to achieve that even distribution. An index of dissimilarity less than 30 is considered low, between 30 and 60 moderate, and above 60 high. After the Civil War, the average indices of dissimilarity for blacks and whites in northern cities ranged from 20 to 45, indicating levels of segregation comparable to those of European ethnics who had recently immigrated. By 1910, however, the average index of dissimilarity in the black ghettos of the largest northern cities had reached almost 60, and in 1940, just before the outbreak of World War II, the average index of dissimilarity in northern cities had soared to almost 90, meaning that 90 percent of African Americans would have had to move from their neighborhoods into white ones in order to achieve perfect integration.

Before 1900, the small numbers of African Americans living in northern cities and the low levels of segregation meant that most African Americans lived in largely white neighborhoods. Whatever poor residential conditions they experienced were due more to discrimination in employment than in housing. A black elite of artisans and professionals was economically tied to the white community, had relationships with whites in power, and generally believed in accommodation with whites, leading, they hoped, to some form of gradual integration someday, a position argued at the time by Booker T. Washington. But the sheer numbers of southern blacks who came north in the first great migration created unique problems.

Racism flared. Employers and white workers sometimes forced skilled black craftsmen to start over as unskilled workers, while factory owners often hired newly arrived blacks as scabs to break strikes and prevent the establishment of unions. Unlike white immigrant strikebreakers, however, black scabs were usually discharged at the conclusion of the strike. The role of African Americans as strikebreakers only increased racial tension between working-class whites and blacks. Bombings and other violence threatened blacks, and beginning as early as 1900 there were massive race riots. Blacks in the "wrong" parts of a city might be attacked; whites who lived in predominantly black areas moved out. Violence at the borders between white and black neighborhoods kept black areas from expanding.

Although the twentieth century's use of violence as a means of maintaining the post–Civil War color line in northern cities crested in the 1920s, it remained a powerful force through the middle of the century and its use declined only gradually thereafter. The fear of violence is still, according to polls, a major deterrent keeping African Americans from moving into white neighborhoods. Although overt violence is now less common, its *threat*—especially the threat that one's children will be harassed or harmed—remains a potent force for segregation.

During the 1920s, whites formed "neighborhood improvement associations," primarily for the purpose of keeping blacks out of their neighborhoods. They lobbied for local zoning restrictions to close hotels and rooming houses that attracted African Americans, and for public investments to keep property values up and thus create economic barriers against black buyers. They organized boycotts against realtors who sold to African Americans or against other businesses that catered to them. Neighborhood improvement associations collected funds to buy back property from black owners and offered cash bonuses to black renters to induce them to leave certain areas. Their most powerful tool was the "restrictive covenant," by which neighborhood whites entered into voluntary agreements that bound signers by force of law not to sell to blacks.

Facing such unified white opposition and antagonism, the black ghetto changed, too. In the first decades of the twentieth century, as levels of segregation increased, a new black middle class made up of businessmen and politicians arose. Their power was born of and depended upon the black ghetto, and they came to oppose the old elite that had favored gradual integration and accommodation with whites. Their new emphasis on racial solidarity and independence found eloquent expression in the writings of W. E. B. DuBois.

The new black politics that emerged differed significantly from the traditional politics of European immigrant groups. As the existence of many a big-city political machine and many an ethnic politician attests, Irish, Jewish, Italian, and German immigrants all relied to some degree on the voting and favor-granting powers to be found in immigrant neighborhoods. Recent studies have, however, shown that these early-twentieth-century immigrant enclaves were qualitatively and quantitatively different from the black ghettos that had formed in most northern cities by 1940.

Since traditional immigrant enclaves bustled with many

nationalities, and since the majority of people with a common ethnic heritage had scattered around the city,[6] ethnic groups historically gained political power, in part, by forging coalitions with each other to realize common goals. These coalitions led to other kinds of mutual cooperation and increased the pace of ethnic integration into the mainstream. This, in turn, meant that ethnic enclaves were but a transitional phase of immigrant assimilation, while under the unrelenting hostility of the larger society ghettos became a permanent feature of black life.

African Americans, therefore, had to find their political power largely in separation. Unlike other ethnic groups, African-Americans' political power came primarily from their ability to vote as a block, under the leadership of powerful black politicians, which meant that those politicians then had a stake in an area's continuing segregation. In effect, if African Americans wanted political power, they had to "take over" a particular area and dominate its politics. Even today, much of African American political power lies in black segregation. Rather than leading to coalitions, this side effect of segregation can often lead to mistrust and, ultimately, political marginalization.

By the early 1930s, the perimeters of the northern black ghetto in most cities had been fixed, and it was difficult, if not dangerous, for African Americans to move into white neighborhoods. Although there were still significant numbers of whites living in black urban neighborhoods, this, too, would change over the next two decades.

The actions of white neighborhood improvement associations, realty practices, and violence along the borders between blacks and whites kept those borders relatively fixed. As more African Americans moved into the ghettos, therefore, pressure for expansion mounted. The prices of property increased so that, paradoxically, property values on the black side of the black-white border were sometimes much higher than those on the white side.

In 1948, the Supreme Court declared residential segregation illegal, specifically outlawing the restrictive covenants that white "neighborhood improvement associations" had used so successfully to keep out blacks. This led to a gradual increase in the permeability of the borders of the ghetto. Permeable borders, however, hardly led to integration, for whites would ultimately begin to move out of neighborhoods if enough (or often *any*) black people moved in. Unscrupulous realtors, taking advantage of white fears, developed the practice of "block busting" within white communities along the borders of the ghetto. The realtor would spread rumors about a pending black "invasion" and peddle fear of declining property values and a black "take-over" of the community. These rumors, in turn, enabled the realtors to buy a few properties from panicked whites at fire-sale prices and then sell them to middle-class blacks brave enough to integrate. Once the rumors were thus given substance, property values fell as other whites hurried to sell and leave. The realtors were then able to buy up the remaining white properties cheaply and sell them to African Americans for exorbitant profits.

The high cost of housing in the ghetto meant that once middle-class blacks had "taken over" a formerly white area, less affluent blacks would move in, leading to further pressure for the more affluent to seek new areas to live in. Thus from the late 1940s into the 1960s, the geographic area of ghettos expanded, while remaining solidly black.

Frequently overlooked in today's rancorous debate about government responsibility for helping the poor are the many ways in which the federal government has subsidized the middle class. The largely middle-class and almost exclusively white suburbanization during the 1950s and 1960s is certainly a case in point. Federally funded road construction made easy commuting from suburban residence to urban jobs possible. FHA and VA mortgage guarantees made home ownership possible. Tax policy allowing deductions on home mortgage interest payments further encouraged ownership. Such government programs and policies were essentially subsidies to the affluent that sponsored white flight. While such flight relieved housing pressure in the cities and therefore allowed for the physical expansion of ghetto areas, it had no effect on the color line, which was maintained despite massive population shifts to the suburbs. Studies have shown that at any moment between 1940 and 1980, whites and blacks lived in essentially separate worlds. It would not be until the Fair Housing Law of 1988 that the federal government gave itself both the mandate and the tools to intervene meaningfully to prevent or at least ameliorate residential segregation.

Whites, of course, can always avoid integration simply by moving out. Studies have shown, in fact, that whites begin to move out of their neighborhoods once the percentage of black residents rises above approximately 8 percent.[7] African Americans, on the other hand, would rarely opt for segregation if given a real choice. While they would not choose to be the *only* black family or one of very few black families in an otherwise white neighborhood, most African Americans would choose to live in integrated communities.[8] The problem, of course, is that once the percentage of black residents reaches a point where most African Americans might feel comfortable moving in, the white population already feels uncomfortable and has begun moving out.

Among the least appreciated of segregation's insidious conse-quences is the *concentration* of poverty that occurs when a popu-lation that is poorer for any reason is also segregated. Because of their history, persistent discrimination against them, and fewer opportunities available to them, African Americans are, as a group, poorer than other Americans. Segregation, therefore, forces African Americans to live in neighborhoods that are more likely than white neighborhoods to have a higher proportion of those who are poor.[9]

The consequences of this concentration can be significant. To take but a single example, where more people in an area are poor, fewer have adequate resources to maintain their property, and buildings soon begin to show small signs of disrepair: a broken window fixed with cardboard instead of a pane of glass, a sagging porch, peeling paint. Other property owners are extremely sensi-tive to these small signs and will view them as signals of decline, leading to reduced incentives to keep up their own properties, which continues in a downward spiral.[10]

Poverty tends to be self-reinforcing, so people born into poor-er neighborhoods have a higher probability of becoming poor themselves.

PUNISHING THE CHILDREN

The concentration of poverty due to segregation has an especial-ly pernicious effect on the educational facilities available to those who live in the ghetto. Because elementary and secondary schools are funded primarily through local taxes, cities with large num-bers of poor people have fewer resources per child and, therefore, less money to fund education. Because ghettos are politically marginalized even within the city, local politicians can more eas-ily neglect education there.[11]

Segregating poor African Americans in the ghetto means, of course, that ghetto schools will be almost completely black and poor. Not surprisingly, then, inner-city children bring more hunger, homelessness, exposure to violence, and other problems to school with them than, say, suburban students, and these "non-educational" problems demand resources that have to be pulled away from already meager educational allocations. Ghetto schools should be getting far more money than suburban schools because the problems they have to deal with tend to be more confounding and deeper. Instead, not surprisingly, they usually get less.

One current approach to improving urban education is the "magnet school," which usually emphasizes a particular area of study like science or the arts, and takes selected students from a district's many schools, grouping together those who have similar interests and abilities. Usually, these schools have more funds, are better staffed, get more access to supplies and equipment, and maintain better physical plants. They are of very significant benefit...to the children who are selected. Ostensibly, children are chosen on the basis of ability, but parents first have to know about the possibility of applying, believe that such a school will be worthwhile, have the time and energy to enter the application process, possess the skills to fill out the written application, and pay the extra fees usually involved. Unfortunately, by skimming off the best students, the most committed or assertive parents, and often a higher-than-average proportion of a school district's budget, magnet schools also make the work of ordinary schools that much more difficult.

A similar weakening of the school system as a whole is the primary danger of any of the proposed educational voucher systems. Although certain demonstration voucher projects have successfully targeted the most difficult inner-city students, any widespread voucher program will also likely to lead to the siphoning off of the better students. Vouchers also threaten to weaken public schools financially. Each voucher usually represents the average amount of money the public school system spends per student. Parents can use it to pay tuition or partial tuition at any school, public or private, that will accept the child. Although not true of all parochial schools, most private schools cost far more than the amount of a voucher for "average public school costs." Poor families unable to afford the added expense will not benefit, nor will the children of parents who, for whatever reason, cannot hunt out alternative schooling, nor will children who cannot get accepted at a private or parochial school. Since voucher money would be withdrawn from public systems, which have large fixed costs in buildings, maintenance, equipment, and teacher contracts, the danger is that the public schools that remain will have even less adequate funding, while having to educate many of the most difficult students who require the highest level of resources.

In its 1896 *Plessy v. Ferguson* decision ratifying the legality of segregation in public facilities, the Supreme Court created the doctrine of "separate but equal." Schools could be segregated as long as the education provided to black students was equal to that provided white students. Justice John Marshall Harlan, in a bitter dissent from that decision, noted that given the social and economic inequality between blacks and whites in the United States at that time, "separate" would never be "equal," a prediction amply realized in the next century. In 1954, in *Brown v. Board of Education*, the Supreme Court recognized the failure of "separate but equal" and demanded the integration of public schools. Almost fifty years later, as Jonathan Kozol has pointed out, we have not only failed to meet the conditions of the 1954 decision, we have also failed to meet the conditions of the 1896 decision. Schools are still largely separate and unequal.

A *Black Alliance for Educational Options* nationwide study released in 2001 revealed that in fifteen of the forty-five largest school districts studied (including New York, Chicago, Cleveland, and Memphis) fewer than half of African-American students graduated from high school with a regular diploma.[12] Without a decent education, a child is handicapped for life.

SICK AND POOR

According to the United States Census, in 2000 over 38 million Americans (14 percent) did not have health insurance *at any time* during the entire year.[13] We tend to assume that if people are poor enough, they are eligible for some kind of governmental health coverage. That assumption is wrong. Less than one-third of the people living in poverty are even *eligible* for Medicaid, the primary form of health insurance available to the poor, and the rate of uninsurance among the poor is over twice as high as among the general population. The low-paying jobs available to poor people rarely offer health insurance coverage as a benefit. It is, of course, out of the question for poor people to purchase health insurance on their own. Even modestly comprehensive family policies currently cost more than $650 a month, half the *total* income of a family of three living at the poverty level, so they remain largely uninsured. This means that in any sort of health emergency the poor must spend a significant percentage of their income on clinic or emergency room visits, especially when young children are involved.

Even those who do qualify for Medicaid must undergo an application process that can be arduous and discouraging. Until the 1996 passage of the legislation known as Welfare Reform, most poor families who received what we usually think of as welfare (Aid to Families with Dependent Children, or AFDC) received Medicaid automatically. Because more than half of these families have been moved off the rolls, they must apply separately for Medicaid, a process that can, in some states, prove virtually impossible for a person who must go to work each day to complete.

Once covered by Medicaid, the poor face a sometimes-insurmountable hurdle: finding a doctor who will accept Medicaid payment. Although patterns vary from state to state, fewer and fewer doctors or hospitals accept Medicaid—largely because reimbursement is usually low—so those who are poor must usually go to hospital emergency rooms or public clinics for their care. But hospitals are not good places to receive routine health care, although they generally handle emergencies well, even for the poor. In fact, federal law requires that any hospital admit and care for emergency patients regardless of ability to pay, but it is now an unusual hospital that offers indigent patients much in the way of continuing care, preventive medicine, or help with routine medical problems. Patients with such problems are increasingly triaged out of emergency rooms. Public clinics can be excellent sources of health care for the patients they accept, but they rarely have the staff or other resources to provide care, much less follow-up, to all who need it. Waits are often long, a different doctor may be seen each time, and there is often no special provision for paying for other needed services like x-rays, lab work, or hospitalization, which can be enormously expensive. And even public hospitals and clinics often try to recoup whatever charges they can from poor clients. So although hospitals may not follow up with aggressive collection routines, patients receive bills anyway.

Thus cost prevents appropriate health care, leading to both poorer health and further poverty. The relationships between health and poverty, however, are complex, for each affects the other. The health of poor people is measurably worse than average: infant mortality, the single most commonly used indicator of population health, is 60 percent greater (and the death rate for newborns is twice as high) for families with incomes below the poverty level than for those above it.[14] Many forms of cancer are more common among the poor.[15] Individuals earning less than $9,000 annually have death rates three to seven times higher (depending on race and gender) than those earning $25,000 or more per year.[16] Poor prenatal care or maternal malnutrition can each lead to learning disabilities and decreased cognitive abilities in children, which in turn can contribute to poor educational achievement, further complicating the experience of poverty.

We know intuitively that poverty can lead to poor health, but research over the last decade has documented that even economic inequality has a separate association with poor health. Studies comparing countries with similar standards of living, for instance, have found that in those with greater levels of economic inequality the health of the entire population (not just the poor) is worse.[17] Similar studies comparing different states in the United States have come up with the same results.[18] The size of the gap between rich and poor matters as well. According to the World Health Organization, the United States, despite its status as the richest country in the world, ranks thirty-second among all nations in the "equality of child survival," a measurement of the distribution of health among different populations within a country. The United States ranks twenty-fourth in life expectancy, and thirty-second in infant mortality,[19] the two most common measures of the health of a population. Over the last twenty-five years, as inequality in our country has increased, we have dropped even further in the rankings. Not only poverty, but also inequality decimates the health of our people.

Examples of poor health among the poor are everywhere: congenital disease and infant AIDS are far more common among the poor, as are the chronic diseases of childhood. Lead poisoning, asthma, malnutrition, anemia, and chronic middle ear infections are not only expensive to diagnose and treat, but can also lead to permanent impairment. Poor children are twice as likely as affluent children to suffer lead poisoning,[20] for instance, and the long-term, deleterious effects on the brain of lead deposits are well known. Severely poisoned children may suffer seizures, coma, and mental retardation, but even those with milder degrees of lead poisoning are at risk for learning and behavior problems. Language acquisition can be delayed, hyperactivity may result, motor coordination may be affected, aggressive or impulsive behavior is more common, and children may have generalized difficulty learning. In addition to being severe problems in their own right, all these symptoms lead to difficulties in school. These difficulties are compounded when the schools in the poor areas lack the capacity to give the individual attention needed; these children may do poorly or drop out altogether. Lead poisoning means that a child enters the challenge of adulthood in the ghetto even less prepared than peers to cope with it.

Childhood asthma has increased dramatically over the last thirty years.[21] Both poverty and inner-city residence are independent risk factors for asthma, and poor African-American children are more than twice as likely to get asthma as other non-poor children and more than four times as likely to be hospitalized. The death rate from asthma is four times higher among African Americans than among whites.[22] Asthma is not only a serious, potentially life-threatening illness in itself, but among chronic health conditions it causes the most school absences. It is the second leading cause of hospitalization for children aged five to nine and may account for a third of all emergency room visits. For the uninsured, the several medications often combined to treat asthma are prohibitively expensive. Asthma becomes highly disruptive to the life of the child and his or her family, adding further chaos to their lives.

While measuring "hunger" is necessarily subjective, the United States Department of Agriculture's annual survey of hunger reports that approximately ten million U.S. households, (accounting for 18 percent of the children) are "food insecure" at some point during the year,[23] meaning that they do not have access to enough food to meet their basic needs. Over three million of these households experience hunger at some point during the year. On any given night, 562,000 American children go to bed hungry.[24] Compared to other low-income children whose families do not experience food shortages, hungry children suffer from over twice as many individual health problems—unwanted weight loss, fatigue, headaches, irritability, inability to concentrate, and frequent colds.

Iron deficiency anemia is also a common result. In the middle-class rural community where I practiced for seven years, anemia was rare. I was shocked, upon moving to the inner city, to discover that well over a third of my young inner-city patients were anemic. Average hemoglobin levels (measuring anemia) were significantly lower than my rural patients'. All of the symptoms of hunger, especially when exacerbated by anemia, mean that hungry children are less able to cope with the difficulties of their environment. School performance suffers, with the expected consequences on future earning power.

Sometimes these health problems exacerbate poverty in surprising ways. Consider middle-ear infections (*otitis media*). Normal acute ear infections cause pain and lead to emergency doctor visits, where they can usually be treated easily. Sometimes, however, *acute* otitis media leads to *chronic* otitis media that may have few symptoms and be detectable only by medical examination. If, as often happens among the poor, the acute, painful episodes are insufficiently monitored through follow-up visits, the chronic otitis media may go undetected. For financial reasons, for instance, a poor child is less likely to revisit the doctor after her acute ear infection seems to have gotten better, so the chronic form remains undiagnosed. This chronic otitis can cause a temporary loss of hearing, which may persist through early childhood. Undiagnosed hearing loss often leads to poor school performance, and so to permanent educational deficiencies, making it that much harder to escape poverty as an adult.

Every illness, of course, makes it more difficult to cope with one's environment, so the poor health status of poor children becomes a permanent impairment. The surround of force seems inescapable.

In addition, the poor are much more likely to live and work in conditions that are detrimental to health. A friend of mine, for instance, cannot afford to move out of her damp basement apartment although the mold spores it breeds severely aggravate her daughter's asthma.

Finally, the stress of simply being poor has been documented to be a real health risk.

The poor get it coming and going.

A SECOND GHETTO: PRISON

Over the last twenty-five years, "law and order" has become a politically potent slogan. The impact of the generally bipartisan demand for "law and order" began to be felt in the early 1980s, when both state legislatures and Congress started to write into law not only lengthier sentences for various crimes, but also "mandatory minimum" sentences. Such laws took from judges the discretion they had previously had in the sentencing process, when they could consider the particular circumstances of the offense committed and of the person who committed it. The result has been a substantial increase in the average length of time served in prison. At both federal and state levels, "three strikes" laws have been passed that mandate sentences of twenty-five years to life for the third felony offense. In states like California, these three strikes can be for relatively minor offenses, including drug possession. More people there have been sentenced under the three-strikes law for simple marijuana possession than for murder, rape, and kidnapping combined, and more for drug possession generally than for all violent offenses.[25] A young man was recently sentenced to a minimum of twenty-five years for his third conviction—this time for stealing a bicycle.

These and other new laws have brought about staggering increases in the size of our inmate population. In 1971, there were fewer than 200,000 people in America's state and federal prisons. By 2001, that number had grown almost to 1.4 million, or close to a seven-fold increase.[26] If local jails, youth facilities, military prisons, and other forms of imprisonment are included, on any given day over two million Americans are incarcerated,[27] a rate of 736 inmates per 100,000 population. This rate is the highest in the world. Only Russia (with a rate of 675 per 100,000) and other countries of the former Soviet Union even come close to our propensity to incarcerate. Other Western democracies average between 55 and 120 per 100,000, that is, between one-sixth and one-twelfth of the American rate. Japan incarcerates only 36 per 100,000, approximately one-twentieth of our rate.[28]

Even these figures pale next to the staggering incarceration rates within the African-American community. In the year 2000, roughly one out of every three black males between eighteen and thirty-four years of age was under the active supervision of the criminal justice system: under arrest, awaiting trial, awaiting sentencing, on probation, in jail or prison, in half-way houses or other mandated programs, or on parole.[29] In Washington, D.C., half of all young black men are currently in the criminal justice system.[30] In nearby Baltimore, it's even worse. These figures include only those currently in the system. If we also count those who have previously been in the system and have now been released, the numbers are even higher. How did this happen? And what has been the impact of these extraordinary incarceration rates on urban life?

The reasons for such high numbers of African Americans in the criminal justice system are complex. Certainly, proportionately higher percentages of poor blacks commit crimes for which we ordinarily send people to jail, especially drug offenses, but also burglary, robbery, assault, and murder. It is also true, however, that we tend to punish the kinds of crimes committed by the poor more severely than similar ones committed by affluent people. Compare, for example, shoplifting and "fudging" on an expense account. Each is a nonviolent crime against business. Since neither source of income is usually reported to the Internal Revenue Service, each is a federal crime. Yet the shoplifter is much more likely to be prosecuted than the executive manipulating his expense account.

Some of the overwhelming increase in incarceration is certainly due to an increase in rates of violent crime between the end of the 1960s, when social conditions in the ghetto began to deteriorate, and 1992, when those rates suddenly started declining, but that's only part of the story. A large part of the increase in incarceration rates over the last generation has had to do with increased length of sentences for less serious crimes. Comparison with European countries supports both explanations. Violent crime levels are generally higher in the United States than in Europe, but it is also true that both our "propensity to incarcerate" and the length of an average sentence for less serious, nonviolent crimes like drug possession or burglary are greater in the United States than in other Western industrial countries. While exact comparisons are difficult to make because crime and punishment statistics in various countries are kept differently, prison sentences in the United States are on average more than two to three times those in European countries for these lesser crimes. Paradoxically, for violent crimes like murder or armed robbery, our sentences—with the notable exception of capital punishment, of course—are closer to those in Europe.

One of the ways in which the criminal justice system weighs more heavily on the poor—especially people of color—is the process of plea bargaining, through which many run-of-the-mill street-crime prosecutions are resolved. In fact, the mandatory minimum sentence that has taken power away from the judge has for practical purposes transferred that power to the prosecuting attorney, who decides not only what charges will be brought against defendants, but also whether or not to prosecute in federal court, where sentencing standards are more severe than in most state courts. Thus, the prosecuting attorney has the authority to offer a plea bargain for, say, a one- or two-year sentence versus facing trial on a charge that might carry a mandatory minimum of twenty years. It often seems in the best interests of even those who are innocent to plead guilty and take the lesser sentence. The lack of time and resources at the disposal of the public defenders assigned to help the poor means a further tilt toward convicting the poor, only adding to the accused's incentive to accept a plea bargain.

There can be no doubt, however, that the war on drugs has been the major cause of the increase in incarceration of black inner-city residents. "Declared" in the early 1980s, the emphasis of this war nationwide has been on law enforcement and the incarceration of drug offenders, not on prevention and treatment. It has also concentrated drug law enforcement on inner-city areas and instituted harsher sentencing policies, particularly for crack cocaine. Thanks to this war (which has in truth been largely a war on the poor), between 1985 and 1995 the number of black state prison inmates sentenced for drug offenses rose by more than 700 percent.[31] In recent years there has also been a dramatic increase in the number of drug cases heard in federal court, as prosecuting attorneys have exercised their authority to bring more offenders under the scope of the more severe federal mandatory minimum penalties.

Once in the criminal justice system, African Americans are usually treated more harshly than other racial groups. The most notorious example is in sentencing for crack cocaine offenses. Crack cocaine and powder cocaine have the same chemical composition, and powder cocaine can easily be transformed into equal weights of crack. Crack, however, is marketed in smaller, less expensive quantities and has, therefore, more often been used by those in low-income and minority communities, whereas powder cocaine is more likely to be used by the affluent. In federal court and in many state courts, the penalty for selling five grams of crack cocaine is the same five-year mandatory minimum sentence as the sentence for selling five hundred grams of powder cocaine. Despite the fact that two-thirds of crack users are white or Hispanic, 86 percent of all offenders sentenced in federal court for crack offences are African American.[32]

Both liberal and conservative criminologists agree that any reduction in drug-related crime caused by our vast increases in imprisonment for drug offenses, while difficult to measure with any certainty, is either small or negligible.[33] Indeed, some have argued that imprisonment makes ex-offenders more likely to use drugs again, because they come out of prison so poorly prepared to reenter society. While the war on drugs has increased incarceration rates for all groups, the increase for black men has been disproportionate. While African Americans are only 12 percent of the population and 13 percent of the drug users, they are 35 percent of those arrested for drug possession, 55 percent of those convicted of drug possession, and an incredible 74 percent of those actually jailed for drug possession.[34]

In other words, an African-American drug user is almost twenty times more likely to spend time in prison for his offense than is any other drug user.

Drug treatment both within and outside the criminal justice system would clearly be more cost-effective in controlling drug abuse and crime than the continued expansion of the prison system. The RAND foundation, a not-for-profit, non-partisan research foundation for the study of military, social, and economic issues, estimated, for instance, that every dollar spent on drug treatment would reduce drug use eight times more than spending the same dollar to expand the use of mandatory sentencing for drug offenders. Similarly, expanding the use of treatment has been estimated to reduce drug-related crime up to fifteen times as much as mandatory sentencing.[35] Studies of drug treatment for the incarcerated have also shown that those who receive drug treatment are significantly less likely to return to prison for another offense than those who do not. Unfortunately, few prisoners receive drug treatment, just as few poor drug users have access to effective drug treatment programs of any sort.

There is no doubt that we need a strong and efficient criminal justice system. There are dangerous people we must remove—at least temporarily—from society. The question is not whether we are "soft" or "tough" on violent crime, but whether the profound increase in incarceration over the last generation has accomplished what it promised. The question is what works and what does not, what will bring real public safety and what only appears to do so. With the deterioration of the social safety net (over the last twenty years government spending for almost every anti-poverty program except Medicaid has decreased) the prison has become our social policy: our employment initiative, our drug treatment program, our mental health policy, our anti-poverty effort, and our program for children in trouble.

In 1997, the latest year for which Justice Department statistics are available, the cost of incarceration to local, state, and federal government was $130 billion,[36] 3.6 times the amount spent in 1982, and these figures continue to increase 8 percent per year. Journalist Christian Parenti reports in his book *Lockdown America* that more than a half-million people work in corrections, making it larger than any Fortune 500 employer except General Motors. Seven billion dollars a year is spent building new prisons. Poor rural areas vie for them and then they immediately become central to the local economy. Five percent of rural population growth between 1980 and 1990 came from prisoners, captured mostly in the cities. Prisons—including the one out of twenty that are private and for-profit—are big business, making it all that much harder, given the ever-greater vested interests in the system, to extricate ourselves from the present morass.

Meanwhile, federal spending on jobs and job training plummets and opportunities for drug treatment disappear. Poverty is correlated with crime, but every extra dollar spent on local, state, and federal penal institutions is a dollar less to spend on the prevention and eradication of poverty. It's not that we don't have other options. Because children who have been abused are far more likely to commit violent crimes later in their life than those who have not, programs working with at-risk families to prevent child abuse have been shown to lower the likelihood of future violent crimes—sometimes dramatically. Timely intervention for young children at risk of impaired cognitive development, behavior problems, and early failure in school can also reduce the likelihood of violent crime, as can programs to intervene in the lives of at-risk adolescents and adolescents who have already had trouble with the law.

There are also enormous hidden costs in our race to incarcerate, costs hidden because they are charged to the ghetto. Keeping half of the young black men in Washington under the supervision of the criminal justice system has devastating consequences. For those actually incarcerated, of course, employment is impossible. One must give up any job one had to go to jail. Most of those on probation or parole are legally allowed to work, but when a criminal record is added to low educational attainment and limited job experience, work proves even harder to come by. Licensing requirements prohibit the formerly incarcerated from some forms of work. Joseph's House, where I work, cares for homeless men with AIDS. A year ago, the City Council passed a law prohibiting any facility like ours from hiring most people with criminal records—even *after* they have served their time. For such men who, under the best of circumstances, would have difficulty finding work, the criminal justice system adds but one more impediment to any attempt to climb out of poverty. Soon, they just give up looking. In the jargon of sociologists, they are no longer "attached to the labor force," and so, in a final irony, they are not even counted among the unemployed, effectively lowering the real unemployment rate. If those incarcerated were counted, the overall unemployment rate for black men would increase by about two-thirds. Many states, in a further gesture of exclusion, prohibit felons from voting, temporarily or permanently. Anyone with a felony conviction for a drug offense is now prohibited from receiving a federal loan for education, making college an even more unrealistic dream.

The imprisonment of some violent offenders, of course, provides benefits to the ghetto community in reduced crime, for it must be remembered that poor-on-poor crime is far more common and far more devastating than poor-on-rich crime. But the benefits of imprisonment for less serious crimes, especially low-level drug selling or possession, are far less clear. Imprisonment also deprives children of fathers, women of husbands and partners, and the community of human resources that could provide positive benefits, including the supervision of young people and other elements of informal social control. As more young people grow up having parents and siblings and friends who are incarcerated, jail time comes to be seen as a normal aspect of the life experience, and the deterrent effect of prison is diminished.

The impact on the ghetto community of this vast increase in the incarceration of African Americans has been devastating.

WORKING—AND POOR

A major change in the face of American poverty over the last generation has involved the loss of the sorts of jobs on which less-skilled workers might have once supported themselves and their families. Between 1963 and 2000, the inflation-adjusted average wage of college-educated men has gone from $38,310 to $53,457, a gain of 37 percent. During that same period, the average wage of men who dropped out of high school has *fallen* from $24,717 to $18,953 (despite a booming economy from 1993–2000), a loss of more than 23 percent, and barely enough to raise a family of four to the official poverty line.[37] The wages of low-skilled women are roughly half those of low-skilled men, although because they were so very poorly paid a generation ago, women's wages have actually risen since 1963. In 2000, for example, the average wage of women who dropped out of high school was $9,996, barely enough to raise a single person—to say nothing of a family—out of poverty.[38]

In the same years, non-wage compensation—primarily health insurance and retirement benefits—has declined for all but the highest-paid employees. The less skilled have been especially hard hit. Few of the jobs available to people with little formal education and limited work skills provide benefits, only increasing the desperation of the situation that the statistics on wages already reveal.

Because of the globalization of the economy, there seems to be a decreased demand for less-skilled workers across the country. Workers in the United States now compete directly with workers in underdeveloped countries, and corporations have too often chosen to move less-skilled jobs out of the country. As a result of decreased demand, wages have declined just as the technological skills required by many companies have risen, leaving the ill-educated, technologically untrained poor behind.

The major policy implication of this profound erosion of wages and compensation among less-skilled workers is that we can no longer count on an expanding economy or even near-full employment to bring people out of poverty. During the 1960s, strong economic growth meant a dramatic fall in poverty as the unemployed went back to work and real wages rose. During the 1980s and 1990s, with similarly strong economic growth, the drop in poverty was minimal. Full-time work no longer guarantees escape from poverty, as the recent results of Welfare Reform have so amply demonstrated. The implications of this fact have not yet registered in government policy.

Three
THE USUAL SUSPECTS

"GHETTO-RELATED BEHAVIORS" AS CAUSES OF POVERTY

Poor people can make poor choices and those choices can aggravate poverty. Living in a highly individualistic culture, most of us tend to blame those individual choices when looking for the cause of someone's poverty. These people still stuck in poverty came from the same social background as *that* one who escaped, we think, so why *shouldn't* I blame them for not making it out? It's easy to slide over not only the structural causes of poverty, but also the important ways in which they interact with and often influence individual choices.

Many residents of ghetto neighborhoods continue to work steadily at whatever jobs are available, despite the almost intolerable pressures of their environment. Often they somehow maintain high aspirations and substantial initiative under conditions that should make either unlikely and under which untold numbers of middle-class, affluent people would quickly falter. Most poor people are not addicted to alcohol or other substances; they do not engage in criminal behavior or traffic in drugs. Despite our society's myths, most of the urban poor are *not* on welfare. They take good care of themselves, their families, and their property. They subscribe to the very values that so many of the rest of us believe are essential: hard work, self-reliance, sacrifice, and respect for others. They are simply poor.

At the same time, there is no denying that one finds in the ghetto disturbingly high rates of unemployment and welfare dependence, addiction and lack of motivation, drug trafficking and other criminal activity. These behaviors seem to be so self-reinforcing that observers have talked of a ghetto "under-class," a group of people whose behavior is virtually incorrigible. The implication is that neither they nor their children have any hope of escaping poverty. It is tempting to look at their behaviors, shrug, and mutter to ourselves, "Well, no wonder they're poor!"

But where do these "ghetto-related behaviors" (as sociologist William Julius Wilson has called them) come from? They are hardly inherent in the black condition, as the first century after Emancipation showed, for during those hundred years of hardship, they were no more prevalent in black communities than elsewhere. (Even single-parenthood, always higher among African Americans than European Americans, was only at 17 percent in 1950, less than the current rate of single-parenthood among whites.) Beginning in the middle of the twentieth century, however, forces beyond the control of individual African Americans led to high rates of joblessness, loss of social organization in the community, a collapse of public education and medical care in the ghetto, and little abatement of discrimination and racism. In this context, ghetto-related behaviors can be seen as understandable responses, some of which may in certain areas be evolving into cultural patterns.[1] These responses perpetuate and aggravate the poverty of the urban poor in a vicious cycle that currently shows few signs of abating.

SINGLE-PARENTHOOD: FAMILIES ON HALF A POVERTY INCOME

An increasing proportion of poor people (especially children) live in households headed by a single woman. Single-parenthood is profoundly associated with poverty. While less than 10 percent of married-couple families live below the poverty line, more than two-thirds of families headed by never-married women (of any race or ethnicity) are poor.[2] Fully half of all families headed by a mother of any race or ethnicity who has never been married have incomes of less than $10,000,[3] an astonishing statistic.

The rate of single parenthood among inner-city black families has grown alarmingly in the last forty years. In Chicago's ghetto areas, for instance, more than five out of six parents aged between 18 and 44 are single.[4] Nationally, more than two-thirds of African Americans' babies are now born to single mothers.[5] Women head over half of all black families, and half of them have never been married.[6] We are witnessing the "feminization of poverty."

Single parenthood clearly contributes to poverty. Most obviously, single parenthood means that there is only one breadwinner in the family, and she must care for the children, as well as work. Despite gains in the last several decades, jobs traditionally held by women still pay less than jobs usually held by men. Furthermore, single parenthood among African-American women (but *not* among white women) is associated with lower levels of education, which means even poorer-paying jobs.

For the single parent, childcare becomes an overwhelming issue. Although costs vary greatly depending upon quality of care, the Children's Defense Fund reports that the average cost for a one-year-old in an urban day-care center is over $5,750 per year in almost two-thirds of the cities surveyed.[7] Families with incomes below the poverty line who paid for childcare spend 23 percent of their income doing so; even such families that get help paying for childcare from relatives or subsidies spend an average of 21 percent of their earnings.[8] (Under welfare reform, families with incomes below and just above the poverty level are supposed to receive government assistance, but nationally only about one in eight eligible children receive such help.)[9] Even with the best childcare, of course, working parents are vulnerable to childhood emergencies that require them to miss work, and poor single mothers cannot afford the best childcare. These mothers become "less reliable" employees, making getting and holding a job yet more problematic.

What about the other parent? Meaningful financial child support is highly unlikely. Less than half of poor single mothers have ever received a child support award in court, and the figure falls to less than a fourth for never-married mothers.[10] Furthermore, only about half of poor single mothers who do get a court award ever see a single payment. Of those few who do receive support, average payment is less than $2,000 per year for all children.[11]

For mothers receiving cash public assistance under the Temporary Assistance for Needy Families program (TANF), the cash assistance program that replaced Aid to Families with Dependent Children (AFDC) in 1996, there is a strong incentive not to report whatever minimal income may be given by the child's father. While rules now vary from state to state, most states have stuck with the previous rule from AFDC: after the first fifty dollars a month, any money reported is subtracted from the public assistance check.[12] There is considerable evidence that many single fathers in the ghetto do not disappear from their children's lives and may take an active part in some aspects of childrearing, but on the basis of in-depth interviews it appears that the amount of money that fathers offer "under the table" is small indeed, averaging thirty dollars per month.[13]

Why is the rate of single-parenthood so high among poor, inner-city African Americans? There is debate about this question and no clear consensus. Although there are some possible factors specific to the black ghetto, society-wide forces have certainly played a major role in this development. In fact, the steadily increasing proportion of births to single mothers (especially to teen mothers), often cited in the media and usually imagined to be largely a black phenomenon, turns out to be largely due to a striking increase of births to single *white* women. From 1980 to 1992, for example, the proportion of births outside of marriage increased among whites by 94 percent, among blacks by only 9 percent.

Social mores have changed considerably. There is now far less stigma attached to having children outside of marriage than there was fifty years ago. Throughout society, social pressures to marry and stay married have decreased dramatically, and divorce rates have soared. Men have felt freer to leave their families.

The extraordinary stresses of ghetto life only multiply the impact of these society-wide factors. Marriage is difficult enough without the problems associated with being poor in America today, so the rate of divorce among the poor is especially high.

High rates of joblessness and low pay for those who do work leave large numbers of inner-city men virtually incapable of supporting families financially, making them less desirable marriage partners.[14] It also tends to be emotionally difficult for such men to stay in relationships when they cannot fulfill the socially expected male role of family breadwinner. Studies show that when a single father has a job, he is much more likely than a jobless man ultimately to marry the child's mother. Of course, the extraordinarily high numbers of young black men locked in the criminal justice system only adds further strains to familial relationships.

Poverty leads to despair. Chronic poverty impairs one's motivation to aspire to something greater than what one sees in the environment. Poverty and despair mean that young men see few options for "proving themselves" other than fathering a child; young women see few options for finding a valued place in the community other than becoming a mother. For many young women (young girls, really), having a child may be the only way of finding someone to love and be loved by. Sex and childbirth among teenagers in the ghetto, then, is more about personal affirmation than about status, a ticket to a better life, or the future. Economic prospects for young, inner-city women are so bleak, regardless of marital status, that there is little reason to value marriage. Desperation can lead to a sense that there is little to lose or that everything is already lost. In fact, a girl from a poor, inner-city family sacrifices only a few of her already limited options by having a child out of wedlock.

Indeed, one aspect of the increase in single-parenthood is usually neglected. We are gradually discovering that the rate of spousal abuse under the stresses of ghetto life is much higher than previously thought. Even though it may be the road to extreme poverty, a woman who fears or expects abuse by her partner may feel herself far better off without him.[15]

This combination of changing societal mores, low pay, joblessness, stress, desperation, despair, futurelessness, and oppression has severely weakened cultural norms in support of husband-wife families and against out-of-wedlock births. In most ghetto communities, there is no longer any stigma attached to having an "illegitimate" baby.[16] Many young ghetto women, in fact, have come to see a man in the house as a liability.

It is important, however, to dispel some of the widespread myths that cling to single parenthood and out-of-wedlock births. One myth identifies welfare payments as a cause of such births. If this were true, one would expect that higher benefits would lead to higher rates of out-of-wedlock births. But a comparison of states with very different levels of welfare payments shows no connection between the size of payments and African-American out-of-wedlock childbearing or teen pregnancy. (Interestingly, there may be a *small* cause-and-effect relationship among whites). Between 1975 and 1990, the real dollar values of welfare and food stamps fell significantly. According to the myth, therefore, there should have been a reduction in the proportion of out-of-wedlock teen childbearing during these years. Instead, the rate nearly doubled during that time period.

Contrary to popular belief, mothers on welfare have, on average, slightly fewer children than other mothers. It *is* likely, however, that the bureaucratic requirements of welfare (such as refusing payments to married couples) have caused some intact couples to stay out of formal marriages.

It is also widely believed that black single women are having more children now than they did forty years ago. Not so. The statistics here can be confusing. The "non-marital fertility rate" of unmarried black women has remained, with some fluctuations, relatively constant: for every 1,000 single women there have been about 100 births per year over the entire period. The rate of single parenthood measures something different, namely the share of all babies born to single women, which has increased sharply among black women from a little more than 20 percent in 1960 to about

69 percent in 1999.[17] The cause of the high rate of single parent-hood in the black community, in other words, is not that individual single women are having more children but that so few women are marrying and that married women are having fewer children.

Single parenthood in the ghetto is a self-perpetuating condition. Since almost all the female role models in ghetto neighborhoods are now single mothers, young women see few other options. Adolescent children of single mothers are more likely to be school dropouts, to receive lower earnings in young adulthood, and to be recipients of public assistance. The single mother can exert less control over adolescents (especially young men), so peer values toward sex, pregnancy, and marriage more easily dominate. It is only a short step to single parenthood as the socially accepted norm.

UNEMPLOYED AND INVISIBLE

One common measure of how well the economy is doing is the unemployment rate. The last few years of the twentieth century saw a sustained unemployment rate of approximately 4 percent, well below what economists had thought *possible* in an economy such as ours. Even among African-American men, the official rates were at historic lows, about 8 percent. But if we break down the statistics by education, it looks a bit different. Among African-American men who had not completed high school, the official rate of unemployment in 2000 (after a decade of an economic boom) was over 14 percent.[18]

Furthermore, the way the unemployment rate is calculated makes it a misleading indicator in poor areas. The only people counted as unemployed are those who are still actively looking for a job, that is, those people who register at unemployment offices. Uncounted are all those too disabled to work, those in prison, those working in the underground economy, and those who have given up even looking for a job.

It is also possible to measure the rates of people "not working," including those in all of the above-uncounted categories. Looking at all American men of working age, 27 percent are not working. Among African-American men, over 35 percent are not working. And among African-American men who have not completed high school, 63 percent are not working. At the end of the longest period of prosperity ever measured, with unemployment at historic lows, five out of eight black men who dropped out of school are not working.[19]

Economists speak of "labor force attachment." Quite obviously, too many inner-city residents—especially men—are *not* attached to the labor force. The problem is a self-reinforcing one. Without a reliable work history, one appears to be a less desirable employee. Once an adult male has been out of work for a significant length of time, he may no longer consider himself part of the work force at all. He sees little chance of ever getting a decent job, and the hopelessness he feels only strengthens his unemployability. He no longer "sees" even the jobs that might be available.

DESCENT INTO HELL

Joblessness and consequent poverty, low levels of education and consequent hopelessness, and segregation and consequent alienation from middle-class norms all combine to create a fertile field for nurturing workers in the drug trade. Young men can earn more in hours than their peers in low-paying jobs do in weeks. Children are recruited as "runners" because of their relative immunity from prosecution, and mothers with no other source of income may look the other way when their sons come home with gifts of money, food, clothing, and other needed items.

With the illegal drug trade comes violence. In addition, during the 1980s and the first years of the 1990s, a staggering increase in the availability of guns, including sophisticated, high-powered, rapid-fire assault weapons, sent the murder rate in the inner cities skyrocketing. As guns became the accepted way of resolving drug disputes, more and more people uninvolved in drug trafficking also acquired and began using them, sometimes for protection, sometimes simply to resolve private disputes.

These weapons have terrorized the wider community. Author Geoffrey Canada, who grew up in an impoverished part of the Bronx and now works with and advocates for youth, reminds us that physical violence has long been a way of settling disputes within the ghetto.[20] Before the proliferation and easy availability of the guns, however, this violence was linked to physical strength, cleverness, courage, and the degree of gang organization, which provided a natural check on the level of violence. Violence was largely a way of establishing a pecking order within a gang or between gangs. Once the new individual in the neighborhood had fought to secure his place, or one gang had demonstrated a convincing superiority over another, a certain tenuous stability would be established that kept the violence under some degree of control. With assault weapons, however, it is not only easier to maim and kill, but it also takes little courage and no strength or skill. Anybody can kill anybody anytime, and there are no natural limits. According to 1998 data, a fifteen-year-old African-American male from Washington, D.C., faced a one-in-twelve chance of being murdered before reaching his forty-fifth birthday.

Although still higher than they were a generation ago, the levels of violence and crime in the cities have fallen dramatically since the mid-1990s. Everyone wants to take credit, of course, and it is not entirely clear what the cause or causes have been. Local police departments, most notably in New York, point to their "zero tolerance" policies, instituted in the early 1990s after some studies indicated that even minor deterioration within a community led to increased crime and violence (the "broken window effect"). Under zero tolerance, people committing minor crimes like loitering or defacing property with graffiti are arrested and prosecuted. Critics, however, have noted that crime and violence rates seem to have fallen just as strikingly and just as fast in cities without such policies. They further note that these policies have led to selective enforcement of laws, with young people of color bearing the brunt of police intervention.

Advocates of the unprecedented expansion of the prison system over the last twenty years have also taken credit, pointing to longer sentences as the major reason for the decrease in crime. And it is likely that just removing certain people from the streets—what criminologists call the "incapacitation effect"—has indeed served to decrease "high-rate offenses" like burglary and robbery, where incapacitation of offenders might make a difference. But closer study of the statistics shows little or no relationship between the severity of a state's laws and decreases in murder, rape, or assault in that state and only a modest effect on the rates of robbery.[21]

There is general agreement that two factors have had at least some role in reducing crime and violence. One is the fading of the ghetto crack epidemic. The popularity of any particular drug has a natural cycle lasting fifteen to twenty years. When cocaine recycled back into popularity in the early 1980s, it entered the ghetto in the form of crack because it was cheap and easy to sell in small doses. But cocaine is a stimulant, and smoking crack leads to especially intense though brief (thirty minutes) stimulation. The intensity of the stimulation leads directly to higher levels of violence, while the brevity of the high puts the addict almost immediately back out in the street needing more. That epidemic has now receded, crack having been replaced again by the depressant heroin, lowering the levels of drug violence.

Most important in reducing crime and violence, however, has been the growth in the economy and the falling rates of unemployment. If one believes that a major cause of inner-city violence is desperation, then an expanding economy—as limited as its effect on the inner city may be—reduces that desperation.

Substance abuse, including a general increase in the use of illicit drugs, is a major problem everywhere in our society, but its damage is especially obvious in the inner city. There, hopelessness and despair are endemic, leading to an intense desire to escape and a sense that one has little to lose. Intoxication provides a seemingly easy, affordable route "out," and drugs are ubiquitous and easily available. Even young children know where drugs are sold. To complete a vicious cycle, as drug use in the ghetto becomes more common, social prohibitions relax. Increasingly, children have addicted people for role models.

Social disorganization and a consequent loss of parental control also help to create a fertile environment for the development of addiction. With less family-imposed structure, young people become even more susceptible to the peer pressure that is everywhere powerful during adolescence. Middle-class adolescents "experiment" with drugs and alcohol, too, and lots of them become addicted. It's more than coincidental, of course, that our language usage has middle-class kids "experimenting" with drugs and using them "recreationally." We use no such mitigating language when speaking about drug use among black ghetto adolescents and young adults.

Finally, of course, affluent people who do become addicted have access to addiction treatment programs not available to those from the ghetto. Most cities do offer some limited kind of public drug treatment program, but these tend to be outpatient programs that send the addict back every night to the very environment that produced the problem in the first place. The few inpatient programs in place are generally too short-term to give sobriety enough time to take hold before the recovering person returns home.

To make addictive behavior even more damaging to poor communities, it has played a major role in spreading that modern plague, AIDS. HIV infection is not, of course, a behavior, but high incidences of drug addiction and sexually transmitted diseases among the urban poor mean that a disproportionate number of those infected with HIV are African American. Difficulties in accessing health care mean that a disproportionate number of them will develop full-blown AIDS. Although African Americans are only 12 percent of the population, they now account for nearly half (47 percent) of new AIDS diagnoses. In the United States in 2000, almost two-thirds of women and almost two-thirds of children reported with AIDS were African American. Among infected young people (ages thirteen to twenty-four) almost two-thirds are African American.[22] While the Centers for Disease Control and Prevention does not break down its AIDS statistics by economic class, its reports make it all too clear that poverty, and not race, is the determining factor in this disproportionate rate of HIV infection among African Americans.[23]

Increasingly, AIDS is becoming a disease of the poor.

"WHY DON'T THEY JUST GET JOBS?"

The poor are frequently criticized for their lack of initiative and motivation, but after eighteen years in the inner city, I must disagree. Most inner-city residents are hard working, scratching out a living for themselves and their families by stacking several part- or full-time jobs at minimal wages one on top of another. In fact, it always surprises me that so many of them are as motivated than as seem to be. Given all the strikes against the poor, any realistic look into the future is bound to seem grim indeed. In the end, though, high aspirations usually collide with the reality of limited vocational options. Like most people in our individualistic culture, the poor ultimately blame themselves for their lack of success, and can easily lose whatever self-confidence they have been able to muster. What little public assistance exists is often administered in ways that make it difficult to move back into the world of self-sufficiency, especially when self-sufficiency is defined as a series of exhausting jobs that don't pay a living wage.

Middle- and upper-class perceptions that ghetto residents lack proper motivation have many sources, not the least of which is our belief that anybody can "make it" in America, which leads directly to the assumption that there must be something wrong with anyone who doesn't. But as their dialect indicates,[24] black inner-city residents are severely isolated from the rest of society and so, not surprisingly, can lack certain social and job-related skills necessary for life in the wider society. If one has seen relatively few people get up in the morning and go to work on a regular basis, if one has not lived in an environment where punctuality is important or necessary, if one has not learned "appropriate" deference toward superiors, if one has not even learned how to deliver excuses in a sincere and believable manner, then one will be misunderstood. Most of us could not say where we learned such skills, but we *have* learned to dress well for a job interview even if the place to which we are applying has few employees who dress well, even if the job we are applying for will not require us to dress well. We will make sure that we are absolutely on time at work each and every day during the first weeks or months on the job, a probationary period during which we know that even reasonable excuses for tardiness are likely to be dismissed. During that probationary period we know we should take few breaks and appear eager to work. If one has not learned such behavioral skills, one's behavior may very well be misread as disrespectful, lazy, or slovenly.

The middle-class perception of many poor people is that "they don't want to work." In my experience, that is rarely the case, but cross-cultural miscommunication is easy.

VICTIMS TO BLAME

The poverty and hopelessness of life in the ghetto make it difficult for residents to develop self-esteem by conforming to the values and ideals of the larger society or to gain prestige in a socially acceptable fashion. When asked by pollsters, many ghetto residents continue to hold to the values of the wider culture, though they may find it impossible to live by them. They consider education important, but inferior schools and other obstacles to formal learning mean that less than half of them graduate from high school and only a fraction go on to vocational school or college.

Marriage has been a goal, but all the issues discussed above lead to single-parent families. People have respect for the law, but for those on welfare bureaucratic rules make staying within the letter of the law virtually impossible, the lack of adequate jobs makes illicit work alluring, and the militarization of law enforcement that turns the ghetto into a battleground foments anger and resentment toward the law and its representatives.

Trying to live up to a set of values without real hope becomes painful. Gradually, within the ghetto, a parallel status system has developed, particularly among the young, in opposition to wider cultural norms. Perhaps oversimplifying, Massey and Denton nevertheless come close to the truth:

> If whites speak Standard American English, succeed in school, work hard at routine jobs, marry, and support their children, then to be "black" requires one to speak Black English, do poorly in school, denigrate conventional employment, shun marriage, and raise children outside of marriage. To do otherwise would be to "act white."[25]

The extent of this oppositional value system varies. Raising children outside of marriage, for instance, has certainly become the norm. Similarly, learning Standard English is not very high on anyone's priority list. On the other hand, only certain subgroups publicly aspire to do poorly in school or avoid conventional employment. The growth of an oppositional value system in the ghetto has received an enormous amount of attention in the media, so the young man lounging on the street corner unwilling to work has become for the wider public the face of the ghetto. But it is also true that, as poverty continues to strangle generation after generation, this oppositional culture has become ever more established, and members of the ghetto who continue to hold the values of the wider society come under increasing pressure to change.

Are individual behaviors an important factor in inner-city poverty? Of course. But historically, the negative structural forces came first and have never gone away. Fifty years ago, before urban renewal and the interstate highway program, before the jobs moved away, before the upper and middle class moved out, before a multitude of societal forces struck with devastating effect, the African-American ghetto was a far different place. In attacking poverty we certainly must confront the realities of "ghetto-related behavior," but we must not become confused about root causes. Mere survival within the "surround" indicates enormous strength and resilience. Observe carefully in any inner-city neighborhood, and you will see many strong, resourceful, independent people who are not only keeping their heads above water but doing their best to strengthen the community as well. The problem is that these people are swimming against an overwhelming current of forces that constantly threatens to overpower even the strongest.

Four

WELFARE IN MODERN AMERICA

There is an enduring myth that earlier in our history government stayed out of the business of welfare. When people were in trouble, according to the myth, extended families and neighbors helped out. When that wasn't enough, charities stepped in to see a person through. Part of the problem today, we've come to believe, is that we depend on the state to do things that family, friends, and charity used to take care of.

In fact, the care of Americans in need has always involved some combination of state aid, private institutional support, and purely voluntary assistance. In both England and colonial America, local governments provided assistance to the destitute, and this practice continued well into the nineteenth century. In order to stave off riots or other civil disturbances, city governments often provided food or shelter during hard economic times. From the beginning, there was public concern about the cost of this relief and its effects on taxes. The publicly supported poorhouses of the nineteenth century were spectacularly unsuccessful attempts to reduce the financial burden on government. Local governments hoped to reduce welfare costs by bringing everyone who required support under one roof and creating economically self-sustaining communities. Far from being self-sustaining, however, the cost of the poorhouses to the government was considerably more than the previous meager welfare payments. Even the federal government got involved in an early form of welfare after the Civil War, offering pensions to veterans of that war and their surviving families. These benefits were later extended to veterans of all wars. The first "widows' pensions" were available to the wives of those veterans. Before the program was discontinued prior to World War I, its cost had risen to 18 percent of the total federal budget, far greater than any comparable program since.

In the late nineteenth century, some employers became part of the welfare state by offering pensions to employees. Later, as part of a "welfare capitalism" movement in the decades before the Great Depression, some larger companies experimented with pensions and other benefits as a way of maintaining company loyalty and retiring older, less productive employees. These benefits could never be counted on, however, because they depended upon the continuing economic health and largesse of an employer. It was only with the growth of unions during the early decades of the twentieth century that employers were brought firmly into the administration of the welfare state through pensions, disability insurance, and health coverage.

But to say that some mixed forms of public assistance have always existed is not to say that they were ever adequate. While some employers have continued to provide good pensions and health benefits, concern that the "undeserving poor" would take advantage of too generous programs and fear that the cost of providing adequate welfare services would be exorbitant have generally left public programs at levels that did little more than keep people from starvation and utter destitution.

WHAT IS "POVERTY"?

We talk glibly of poverty without defining our terms, but definitions are important. In this book what I mean by poverty is having an income below the federally determined poverty level. This is the official definition and the one most commonly used in the United States. It is important to be aware, however, that this official poverty level severely understates the actual number of people who live in what most Americans would intuitively consider poverty.

The "official poverty level" first seeped into government parlance in 1961, when Mollie Orshansky, a staff analyst at the Social Security Administration, needed an objective definition for statistical work she was doing. She reasoned that the financial inability to purchase an adequate diet would be generally considered poverty. In the 1950s, the United States Department of Agriculture (USDA) estimated that the average American family spent about a third of its income on food. Every year the USDA also estimated the cost of a minimally adequate diet. Orshansky, therefore, defined the poverty level as the cost of a minimally adequate diet multiplied by three. That definition stuck, and without real evaluation became the official government standard, which is revised annually, using updated USDA estimates of food costs. Although levels are calculated for various family sizes, when used by itself the term "poverty level" usually refers to the amount a family of four would need to stay out of poverty, which in 2001 was $17,650.

Unfortunately, Orshansky's definition is too simplistic for the weight it has had to bear over the last forty years. There are numerous problems. First, the poverty level is held to be the same throughout the continental United States, although the cost of living varies enormously. Someone living on a farm in South Carolina needs less money to live than a person living in the inner city of New York.

Second, non-cash income like food stamps and housing subsidies was only minimally available in 1961 and is, by definition, excluded from the calculations. A family with an income just below the poverty line who receives food stamps and a housing voucher is clearly better off than another family with an income just over the poverty line who receives neither of these benefits, but the former is considered poor and the latter is not.

Third, taxes are not taken into account, so neither the expense of taxes or the income of the Earned Income Tax Credit changes one's "income" for purposes of the calculation.

But by far the biggest problem with the poverty level is that it is obsolete. Relative costs of different expenses have changed significantly in the past fifty years. Utility costs have risen faster than the cost of food, as have housing costs. A one-bedroom apartment in the Washington, D.C., area (at the government fair market rent of $716) would be 61 percent of the poverty level income for a family of three. If food still costs 33 percent of their budget, that leaves only 6 percent or $71 a month for all other expenses, including childcare and health care. Technology—washers, dryers, kitchen appliances, television, computers—now eats up a larger portion of expenditures. Probably the biggest single issue, however, is childcare. Because most women with children stayed at home in the 1950s, the cost of childcare, now significant for young families, is still not included in the calculation.

Such changes mean that the average American family in 2001 spends closer to one-fifth of its income on food, so it would be reasonable to reset the poverty level by multiplying the least expensive food plan by *five* not three, but this would more than double the number of people we would consider poor.

Unfortunately, the determination of the poverty level has deep political implications. Raising the poverty level to define more people as poor, for example, would boost the arguments of those who want to spend more to ameliorate poverty; lowering the level would support those who believe we are already doing enough. Statisticians both inside and outside the government have suggested a system that would be more consistent, that is, that would take into account government benefits, the cost of childcare, taxes, earned income credits, and so on. The political implications of redefinition, however, are so loaded that most proposals recommend standardizing any redefinition so that the new number of people considered poor would be equal to the number under the old system. There would be no attempt to reach some kind of consensus as to who should really be called poor.

There can be no doubt, however, that for those who live in the cities, where costs are invariably higher than in rural areas, the official poverty level severely underestimates poverty.

WHAT (AND WHY) IS "WELFARE"?

The term "welfare" properly means *any* form of institutional or state assistance to people in need. Local relief payments, disability payments, medical assistance, cash aid to families, food stamps, housing vouchers, and assistance to the elderly are all examples of state-financed welfare. Welfare also includes health insurance and pensions offered by employers, and similar elements of what might be called "the private welfare state." In the current political debate, however, the term "welfare" has popularly been limited to that form of federal/state public assistance given to single mothers and their families, previously known as Aid to Families with Dependent Children (AFDC). In 1996, under what is now called Welfare Reform, AFDC was dismantled and the money bundled in "block grants" and given over to the state governments for the administration of a new program, Temporary Assistance for Needy Families (TANF). Restricting the discussion of welfare strictly to "cash assistance to poor families," however, tends to hide the extent of the patchwork American welfare state that does exist and to distort our understanding of the changes that have occurred over the last generation. Direct cash assistance to families through TANF, for instance, is not the only element of welfare successfully attacked and either eliminated or reduced during the last generation.

We think of welfare's purpose primarily as the alleviation of poverty, but both public and private welfare have other functions as well. Public assistance programs promote social order and discipline. Government can initiate or expand assistance programs in attempts to appease political protest or unrest, such as Congress's mandated increases in AFDC benefits after the inner-city riots of the 1960s. Similarly, the state can restrict or withdraw programs in an effort to discipline the poor, for example the recent attempts by several states to control childbearing among the poor by refusing to offer TANF benefits for additional children born to women already on the program. Private welfare benefits have also sometimes been offered in specific response to worker unrest or union organizing efforts. Welfare, and the stigma attached to it, has also been used to frighten working people into accepting without protest low wages and difficult working conditions.[1]

Welfare has perhaps most commonly been used as a mechanism for political mobilization. Particularly in local politics, public officials have frequently used public assistance as a reward for political support. Chicago's Democratic political machine, for example, long wielded this form of patronage as part of its effort to maintain its power base. Ronald Reagan, on the other hand, used his *opposition* to welfare as a strategic part of his presidential campaigns in 1980 and 1984, reciting anecdotes of "welfare queens" fraudulently receiving multiple checks and driving new Cadillacs.

Since 1960, welfare benefits have been used in the attempt to make up for past racial injustice. Although Lyndon Johnson's War on Poverty began as a program directed at white Appalachian poverty, many of its resources were quickly diverted to fight black urban poverty. This was in part due to a fear of urban riots, but for many leaders was also a conscious effort to respond to the Civil Rights movement and represented a heightened consciousness of racial discrimination.

Each of these purposes is still operative in the current debates over welfare.

The debate about who "deserves" public assistance dates back at least five hundred years to the beginnings of modern welfare in Europe. Societies have always tried to separate those who suffer through no fault of their own from those who have apparently brought their difficulties upon themselves due to substance abuse, laziness, unwillingness to work, promiscuity, or any other trait deemed undesirable at a given historical moment. The English 1531 Act for the Punishment of Sturdy Beggars, for instance, was among a number of early laws that denied charity to the able bodied. As a matter of policy, American society has generally tried to confine private charity and governmental assistance to the "deserving," while insisting that the "undeserving poor" improve their character as a condition for receiving relief.

The problems with this unending debate are several. It is, in practice, impossible to distinguish with any certainty the "deserving" from the "undeserving," no matter how defined. If society tries to enforce such a separation through governmental rules and regulations, it quickly discovers that the causes of poverty are complex and sometimes subtle, and that decidedly difficult-to-determine psychological conditions heavily influence judgments of "deservingness." A person who, on paper, looks lazy and unwilling to work, for example, may, on closer examination, be mentally or emotionally incapable of performing any useful work. It is almost impossible to make these distinctions accurately and consistently through formal regulations. But if society tries to separate the "deserving" from the "undeserving" through subjective personal interviews and one-on-one determinations, local prejudices weigh far too heavily for the overall process to be considered either just or accurate.

In addition, framed this way, the debate over who is to be helped will largely ignore the structural causes of poverty examined in this book, while the very impossibility of separating the "deserving" from the "undeserving" will insure that any regulations and policies designed to weed out the latter make life unjustly miserable for the former. Those who ran nineteenth-century poorhouses, for instance, were afraid that "undeserving" people would overrun their institutions. In most cases, the institutions responded to this threat by making life in the poorhouses so miserable that no one would want to stay, were any other choice available. That probably succeeded in keeping out most of the "lazy" people (whatever their actual problems), but at the cost of brutally punishing those who had no other recourse. A current example of this attitude that punishes the needy for fear of making the program too attractive is the level of TANF benefits, which are so low that no one could survive on them. Although benefits differ from state to state, the average maximum payment for a family of three in 1999 was $394 per month or $4,728 per year, approximately one-third of the official poverty level. In Alabama, TANF payments to a family of three with no other income were $164 a month, less than one-sixth of the official poverty level.[2]

As might be expected, the definition of who is "deserving" has changed over time. Not so long ago, for example, poor single mothers with young children were considered "deserving," while we now consider most young welfare mothers "undeserving" of any ongoing assistance.

OFF ON THE WRONG FOOT

Those aghast at the low welfare payments and other elements of our contemporary tattered safety net are tempted to look back with nostalgia at the New Deal of President Franklin D. Roosevelt, a program rightly considered the beginning of the modern American public welfare state. In fact, however, the seeds of the current confusion over social welfare were sown during Roosevelt's administration. We will only understand today's poverty if we understand the history of social welfare, beginning with the New Deal.

Aside from the veterans' and widows' pensions that ended before World War I, the federal government was rarely involved in welfare until the Great Depression of the 1930s and Roosevelt's administration. Millions of middle-class families were suddenly thrown into poverty. "The poor" had become "us." Political attitudes toward welfare changed almost overnight, and there was great demand for federal assistance to those suffering from poverty. Roosevelt quickly created the Federal Emergency Relief Administration, which distributed approximately $18 billion in direct relief from 1933 to 1936. His administration also created work for the unemployed. Beginning in 1933, the Civilian Conservation Corps often sent unskilled men aged eighteen to twenty-five to mostly rural work camps. At its peak it employed more than half a million men. Another program, the Works Progress Administration (WPA), recruited workers of all sorts, ranging from unskilled laborers who worked building highways to photographers sent out to document the devastation of the dustbowl. At *its* peak the WPA employed more than three million people. Despite the size of these programs, they served less than a quarter of those eligible for relief.

Both of these programs were ended when World War II transformed the glut of workers into a shortage, but a number of programs initiated during the Depression became cornerstones of America's "social insurance" system. Although these have proved powerful anti-poverty programs in their own right, they differed from public assistance in that they were not targeted specifically to the poor, but covered the whole population. As a start, a set of largely voluntary unemployment insurance programs that, prior to the Depression, differed from state to state, was transformed under the 1935 Economic Security Act into a mixed federal-state unemployment insurance program in which the federal government mandated uniform standards that the states were primarily responsible for enforcing. Employers were required by state law to pay premiums for certain levels of unemployment insurance that would then provide a cushion for people who lost their jobs.

The most important of Roosevelt's innovations in social insurance, however, was probably the Social Security program, also a part of the Economic Security Act of 1935, which provided benefits not only for the elderly, but also for the disabled. Although the program initially excluded agricultural workers and domestics (and therefore most African Americans), it has since been significantly expanded. Sold to the public as a pay-as-you go *insurance* program, Social Security has nevertheless also always been a welfare program, that is, a wealth transfer in which payments by younger, working individuals provided benefits for the retired and disabled. Its nature as a welfare program becomes clear if one considers that most beneficiaries have, up until now, received approximately twice what they would have received if their payments had simply been invested in United States Treasury bonds, and that—compared to their contributions—poorer individuals receive proportionately more than do wealthier.

Perhaps the greatest indication that Social Security is actually a massive welfare program is the amount of money in the trust. Any true insurance program should be able to stop taking in new business today and still have enough money to meet all of its future obligations. This has never remotely been the case with Social Security, which, at the end of 2000, had $931 billion in its trust fund and liabilities of $9.6 *trillion* (or $9,600 billion). Social Security has always been a transfer of income from working people to certain people who were not working, not a true insurance program.

The program was significantly strengthened with markedly increased benefits during the 1960s. Nothing indicates its enormous success more clearly than the 1997 poverty rate for the elderly—just over 10 percent. That same year, the poverty rate for children, who have no such program, was twice as high. It is estimated that in the absence of Social Security payments, 50 percent of today's elderly would be poor.

In the Economic Security Act of 1935 there was also a matching grant program that encouraged states to assist the elderly who had not worked long enough to collect benefits under Social Security. Because the program was administered by the states, its benefits varied greatly from state to state and were usually not sufficient to live on. Nevertheless, such limited old-age assistance, which did not discriminate as much against African Americans, was, for the most part, what most Americans thought of as "welfare" until the mid-1950s.

The New Deal cemented into place the ultimately untenable distinction between "social insurance" and "public assistance" that has, in the end, prevented the United States from developing a more comprehensive program of economic security similar to those in Canada and the countries of Western Europe. In the United States, we consider programs like Social Security, Medicare, disability pensions, and disaster relief to be social insurance. All of us pay in and, in times of trouble, any one of us can take out. Usually, there is no stigma attached to taking help from a social insurance program; we think that that's what it's there for and that we should take it if we need it. Yet we consider payments to families with young children, food stamps, general relief, and Medicaid to be "public assistance," akin to charity, undeserved handouts given by a generous "us" to a handicapped or malingering "them." Stigma is built in: public assistance programs seem to us to be only for those who just do not have what it takes to succeed. By calling a program public assistance, we assume the likelihood that someone undeserving of help will try to cheat. In fact, social insurance and public assistance are both forms of wealth transfer. Resources are taken from certain groups of people (those who are working) and provided to other groups (largely those who are not).[3]

It is no coincidence that social insurance programs are administered by the federal government using nationally uniform standards and benefits pegged to inflation. Public assistance programs, on the other hand, tend to be administered by state or local governments, with standards that vary from place to place, while cost-of-living raises for public assistance programs generally depend upon the uncertainties of local legislative whims and processes. Since few state or local governments permit "deficit spending," in times of recession, when the need for public assistance is highest, local and state tax coffers dwindle. As a consequence, federally administered "social insurance" programs have substantially better benefits than "public assistance." Compare the average $394 TANF payment for a family of three to the usual $515 payment for a *single* disabled person covered by the federal SSI program. As another example, in the twenty years *before* the Welfare Reform Act of 1996, AFDC benefits (adjusted for inflation) declined by 40 percent, while Social Security benefits remained stable.

PARTIAL SOLUTIONS

The administrations of Lyndon Johnson and—contrary to popular perception—Richard Nixon saw the next major expansion of federal social insurance. The War on Poverty, as Johnson called it, aimed to eradicate poverty in the United States. It was a time of national self-confidence: if we could put a man on the moon, surely we could end poverty. The Johnson administration, however, was unwilling to challenge the essential societal structures responsible for such extreme inequality. Instead, its programs stayed within the conceptual separation of social insurance and public assistance codified in the 1930s.[4]

Johnson's programs were grandly conceived; they led to a significant increase in spending for social welfare. Unfortunately, the war in Vietnam intervened, and funding for almost every program was severely curtailed. According to Michael Harrington, the "war at home" never cost even one percent of the federal budget, making it more a skirmish with, rather than a war on, poverty. Despite their limited funding, however, many war on poverty programs were successful by almost any measure. The Headstart program, which provided preschool childcare and instruction; Legal Aid, which offered legal services to those who would otherwise be unable to afford one; the Job Corps, which provided jobs and training for young people; and Volunteers in Service to America (VISTA), which recruited volunteers for service in poor areas, offered services that demonstrably improved the lives of many. Food stamps—begun as a small program during the New Deal to supplement farm income, revived in 1961 by John F. Kennedy, and vastly expanded by Nixon to make stamps available without cost to the poor—successfully protected people from hunger. Increases in disability payments prevented destitution, Medicaid quite successfully brought medical care to those below the official poverty level, and Medicare provided for the elderly and permanently disabled. Social Security benefits were raised and, in 1972, indexed to inflation, ultimately cutting the poverty rate of the elderly by two-thirds and making the elderly the least poor American age group.

A common perception is that the Great Society programs failed, a conclusion that ignores the evidence of their successes. Part of this misperception arose because many of the programs were evaluated as failures using goals that were either never intended or never even barely reachable based on the limited funding available. For example, the intent of AFDC payments was to provide some financial relief to struggling families. Even at their height during the 1960s, the levels of AFDC payments were never high enough to bring people out of poverty. In fact, given the policy of subtracting private sources of income (such as gifts or part-time jobs) from AFDC benefits, and given that official poverty rates are calculated before taxes and do not count in-kind income (such as food stamps), it's not even *theoretically* possible for AFDC benefits to raise a family above the poverty level. To judge AFDC a failure because it did not lower poverty rates, then, is to misunderstand the purposes of the program. To take another example, evaluating Medicaid by its goal—to make health care accessible to the needy who are eligible for it—reveals a highly successful program. Headstart and the Job Corps were, judged by their own goals, also very successful. Although it is difficult to separate out the effects of the War on Poverty from those of the economic expansion that took place at the same time, poverty did decline sharply throughout the 1960s. Twenty-two percent of the population fell below the official poverty line in 1960, only 11 percent in 1973.[5]

"Community action programs" were controversial from their inception in 1964 and were responsible for much of the backlash against the War on Poverty. The programs implicitly defined powerlessness as an important source of poverty. To empower poor people, the federal government funded community activists directly, thus deliberately bypassing local politics and politicians, whom federal antipoverty officials often saw as part of the problem. Local community action agencies deliberately recruited members of target communities as leaders and employees, often alienating local officials even as they empowered neighborhood groups. A few highly publicized examples of local African-American recipients who used funds to support militant tactics, however, created a backlash against not only the programs themselves but also the War on Poverty in general. Although community action agencies changed local politics in often-positive directions, they created too many enemies, and in 1967 Congress amended the law to require local government approval of the agencies. In 1974, funding was completely withdrawn.

The expansion of the AFDC program in the Great Society era represented a major change in social welfare policy. From its beginnings during the New Deal, AFDC had, in practice, been confined mostly to widows with dependent children. In the 1960s, however, a combination of factors—the growing feminization of poverty, a more militant welfare rights movement, the soaring promises of the War on Poverty, and a sense after the first of the urban riots that something had to be done—resulted in drastically increased applications for assistance, mostly from women who were divorced, separated, or never-married, rather than widowed. This change was due neither to an increase in the number of the poor nor to changes in the law that made more people eligible, but rather to the fact that more eligible people applied and more applicants were accepted. At the beginning of Johnson's presidency, only one out of three eligible families received AFDC. By 1971, more than nine out of ten eligible families were receiving benefits. Although AFDC has always supported more white than black families, a popular perception grew that this program—what most people think of as "welfare"—primarily supported inner-city black families

In recent years, those arguing for "welfare reform" have claimed that the costs of "welfare" had spun out of control, blaming AFDC by implication. In fact, however, AFDC costs had declined since the 1960s. It was the Medicaid program, which provides matching grants to states to encourage medical assistance to the poor, whose costs had soared. Before AFDC was dismantled in 1996, Medicaid expenditures had become almost five times as expensive as AFDC.

Medicaid costs ballooned over the past several decades primarily for three reasons. First, the cost of medical care has risen precipitously and across the board. Second, though Medicare (publicly run health insurance for people over sixty-five and most permanently disabled people) covers most kinds of medical costs for the elderly, it only covers 80 percent of those expenses and does not cover nursing home care at all. As a result, Medicaid must take on medical care not only for poor mothers and their children, but also for the disabled and the elderly poor. Medicaid has certainly stepped into this breach, but the cost of nursing home care has risen even more rapidly than other medical expenses. (The majority of those who receive Medicaid's nursing home benefit are formerly middle-class elderly who have run through their savings paying for the costs of their care.) Although two-thirds of Medicaid recipients are young women and their children, they account for less than one-third of its payments; the remainder goes to the disabled and elderly. Finally, costs have risen because the program has been an "entitlement," meaning that the government has legally committed itself to provide whatever funds are necessary to cover anyone who fits the guidelines. Even so, nationally only about a third of those living below the official poverty line have been eligible for its benefits.[6]

The ballooning costs of Medicaid account for almost all the increased federal expenditures on social programs for the poor over the last twenty years. Almost every other program has actually contracted, while—for reasons that its recipients have no control over at all—Medicaid has grown enormously.

By far the most massive of the social welfare programs during the Johnson and Nixon administrations were Social Security and Medicare. While these programs were not directed specifically toward the poor, they were and remain the most effective federal antipoverty programs. The Great Society expansion of Social Security and creation of Medicare—from which *everyone* benefited—dwarfed funding for all other social welfare programs combined. It is not coincidental that these two programs were so important in alleviating poverty. Because they targeted everyone of a certain age, they enjoyed broad political support. Not only were they adequately funded, but (unlike AFDC, for example) their benefits also increased *automatically* with inflation. As a result, however, the federal government spent about 75 percent of its social welfare budget during the Johnson and Nixon years on the non-poor!

Although it is not well known, social welfare programs expanded greatly under Richard Nixon, the Republican president who followed Lyndon Johnson. Despite Nixon's anti-welfare rhetoric, government spending on welfare and public housing actually increased more during his administration than in Johnson's.

WAR ON WELFARE

Although the Great Society programs were moderately successful, given their funding levels, the seeds of a powerful backlash had been sown. The war in Vietnam not only drained billions of dollars from the federal budget that might otherwise have gone into public assistance programs, but "Johnson's war" also claimed much of the president's energy and undermined his authority in other areas. The debate over the war divided the Democrats into feuding camps and emboldened conservative opponents.

In addition, the soaring rhetoric that went with the largely underfunded Great Society programs raised unreasonable expectations. Americans had not grasped the depths of poverty in the country and believed the promises to end it. Although Johnson's programs were not, in fact, specifically targeted at black, inner-city communities, media coverage certainly helped shape a general perception that the intended beneficiaries were African Americans. When the northern ghettos erupted in the second half of the decade, support for the Civil Rights movement—and along with it the War on Poverty—declined precipitously. In addition, rates of crime rose sharply during the second half of the 1960s, probably more because the Baby Boomer generation was coming into its adolescence,[7] than due to the expanding ghettos. Whatever the explanation, the national mood changed from one of sympathetic concern to fear and mistrust. "Law and order" became a driving concern for many in the middle class. Increasingly, the public came to feel that the disadvantaged needed to be controlled rather than "coddled."

The Great Society programs had been passed during an era of economic expansion and prosperity that looked as if it might continue forever. The popular sense had grown that the country could both fight poverty and, at the same time, increase individual workers' living standards. In 1973, however, the oil embargo burst that fantasy, creating apprehension and economic uncertainty. Unemployment and skyrocketing inflation stoked fears of scarcity. African-American despair in the inner city was highly visible (on television, if nowhere else), and growing rapidly.

White voters, even those many who had no contact whatsoever with black communities, found this threatening. Welfare and its urban clients became excellent scapegoats for the increasing decline in American productivity.

By the mid-1970s, the perception had grown that, to borrow Ronald Reagan's later phrasing, "we had declared war on poverty and poverty won." Conservative critics blamed the poor for their poverty, blamed welfare for exacerbating it, offered volunteerism as a better response than "government handouts," and pushed government at all levels to reduce benefits. In part due to the fiasco of the Moynihan Report and in part due to fear of the black, inner city itself, liberal voices had withdrawn from the debate over black urban realities, so the conservative argument went unopposed. The political mood shifted dramatically. Government—from local to federal—has waged war on welfare ever since.

As economic realities in the large cities of the North and Midwest worsened in the mid-1970s, their tax bases declined—this at the very moment that the need for services was increasing. As cities' infrastructures began to collapse, their credit ratings slipped. Rural and suburban voters drew back even further from urban problems, and felt even less responsibility for spending state money on urban problems, less willing to "subsidize" urban deficits. Voters in most states, for instance, rescinded their support for general relief to the destitute, which disproportionately affected those large cities. Aside from food stamps, such general assistance programs, which gave low levels of direct cash aid, had been the sole source of government assistance to most financially needy adults who were neither parents of small children nor disabled. (By 1998, only four states remained that gave direct cash assistance to able-bodied adults without dependent children.)

As many affluent left urban areas, cities lost more political power. The "New Federalism" of the Reagan and first George Bush administrations sharply cut direct federal aid to the cities. By 1980, federal assistance came to 18 percent of urban budgets; by 1990, it accounted for only 6.4 percent.[8]

During the 1980s, as federal and state governments were reducing their contributions to urban areas, the cities were hit with the explosion of crack cocaine addiction and its associated violence, the AIDS epidemic and the public health costs that went with it, and the growing problem of homelessness. As a result of their troubled status and the tax-cutting mood of the country, most city governments were forced to adopt austerity budgets. Since other government functions like road maintenance or trash pickup require a relatively constant level of funding, and still other functions like police protection are unlikely to be cut in a time of social crisis, social welfare budgets suffered disproportionately. Cities were forced to cut social services and other forms of assistance. General relief, housing assistance, local medical assistance (to that majority of the indigent not eligible for Medicaid), child protection, and other social service programs were decimated.

State and local governments often chose to reduce spending by tightening eligibility requirements. Most benefits had previously been given to people on the basis of need alone. If you were poor enough, you received benefits. During the 1970s, states and cities began restricting eligibility to those considered "unemployable." Although the definition of "unemployable" varied from locale to locale, the restrictions generally meant that childless, able-bodied adults were no longer eligible for help. It did not matter whether or not there were appropriate job openings available. Those who were physically capable of working were denied benefits even if they looked for and could not find work. Local governments also changed eligibility regulations to exclude those who were unable to work because of alcoholism or drug addiction. Once again, government charged itself with discriminating between the "deserving" and the "undeserving" poor. Hundreds of thousands of people lost their eligibility, and benefits for most others declined.

The federal government also took an active role in the attack on welfare. In 1980, Ronald Reagan was elected president in a campaign that featured fierce anti-welfare rhetoric. He promptly set about trying to dismantle welfare programs. His administration attempted to cut not only AFDC, but also elements of social insurance. A strong negative public reaction, however, immediately precluded significant changes in Social Security or unemployment insurance, a clear example of the political popularity of programs perceived to be "social insurance," not "public assistance."

The administration was more successful, however, in cutting into disability insurance, part of the Social Security Act intended for anyone who had been disabled for at least a year. Charging fraud and waste, the administration tightened requirements (a move that required no approval from Congress) and speeded up the mandatory regular review of cases. Of the 400,000 cases "reviewed" in the first year of this accelerated process, almost half were ruled ineligible for further benefits. When those denied had the legal resources to challenge their administrative termination, over half of them had their eligibility reinstated on appeal. The majority of those cut, however, never challenged and simply lost eligibility.

Public assistance programs were even more successfully targeted. By 1983, 300,000 families had lost their eligibility for

AFDC, "saving" the government over a billion dollars a year. Eligibility was restricted and benefits reduced for food stamps, school lunch programs,[9] Medicaid, extended unemployment benefits, and other programs. The federal housing budget was slashed from $74 billion in 1987 to less than $13 billion in 1989,[10] virtually precluding any new housing construction for the poor. Not surprisingly, homelessness soared in the next decade.

By 1992, political support for curtailing social welfare programs was bipartisan, and in most places it was political suicide to campaign on the basis of increasing the amount the government spent on programs for poor people. The welfare reform legislation that Congress passed in 1996 was only the capstone on this decades-long process.

THE MYTH OF THE WELFARE QUEEN

Except in certain low-cost-of-living areas in high-benefit states (for example, rural areas of Minnesota), it has never been remotely possible to survive on AFDC or TANF benefits alone. Even adding food stamps does not bring a family anywhere near the official poverty level, not to mention the 150 percent of poverty level that a family really needs to survive. Those receiving government assistance, therefore, have to find other sources of income.

How do they do it?

Most of us get only anecdotal information about welfare and people who are poor. We ingest the media's sensationalized stories. We listen to acquaintances who work as police officers, social workers, or other kinds of "street-level bureaucrats" dealing directly with those among the poor having the most difficulty. We ourselves observe men loitering on street corners or young women using food stamps at the grocery store. We don't pay much attention to statistics or studies. As a result, our perceptions have been systematically distorted in negative ways. Common beliefs about welfare and work reflect these distortions.

We hear much about "welfare-to-work," as if one were either on welfare *or* working. The common association is between welfare and laziness. Nothing could be further from the truth. Many people on welfare work—they have to in order to live.

Before writing *Making Ends Meet*,[11] sociologist Kathryn Edin and anthropologist Laura Lein asked 379 welfare mothers from four different cities about their survival strategies.

The first jolt to our preconceptions is that these welfare mothers tended to spend less money than poor people with similar incomes who had full-time jobs. In part this was because working mothers have extra expenses like childcare, transportation, and clothing, but even when these expenses were taken into account, welfare mothers apparently lived more frugally. Contrary to myth, they managed their money well. Nevertheless, their total benefits averaged about 60 percent of their expenditures. It should be no surprise, then, that all these welfare families had some other source of income.

These other sources of income fell into three main categories. The first was work. Almost half of the welfare mothers interviewed worked, averaging $276 a month in earnings. Although reporting those earnings to their social worker is legally required, few of them did so, since almost all of their reported earnings would have been subtracted from their welfare checks, leaving them more exhausted and no further ahead financially. Most of the work they did was informal: babysitting, yard work for friends, or working for a small business that would pay in cash under the table. Only a small minority (about 8 percent) worked in the underground or illegal economy, chiefly at prostitution or drug selling.

Their second major source of income was friends and relatives, including boyfriends and the fathers of their children, whether they lived in the house or not. Almost four out of five welfare recipients received such support from their personal networks, although, for the same reasons, most did not report this income. From the women's stories, however, these contributions were hardly "free money." These mothers had to provide something in exchange for what they received: time and energy in maintaining relationships, free babysitting, house cleaning. Boyfriends who provided money received room and board in exchange.

The third source of extra income was local charity. In most cases, this was not considered a desirable source because few charities could offer much. Going from one to the other and meeting various requirements, only to receive a grab bag of groceries or some second-hand clothes, ate up time and energy.

The take-home lesson Edin and Lein offered was that virtually all welfare mothers "work" in many senses of the word: they do extra jobs, maintain the networks that support them, visit charities, and continually strive to meet the bureaucratic requirements necessary to stay on AFDC or TANF itself.

As if to prove the point about how deeply embedded our misconceptions are, a front-page article in the *Washington Post* quoted extensively from Edin and Lein's research, but managed to look past the reality that the women interviewed *had* to find some other source of income in order to survive. It looked past their industry and resourcefulness and past the fact that they are not lazy to make a darker and more ominous point: these women were committing welfare fraud![12]

THE END OF WELFARE

Most people agree that welfare needed reforming. Because AFDC was a federally funded but state-run program, benefits varied wildly from state to state, ranging from 12 percent to 55 percent of the poverty level for a family of three, making it not only an inadequate but also an inequitable program. In addition, AFDC contained perverse anti-work and anti-marriage incentives. Essentially all work income was deducted from benefits, and mothers going to work also lost Medicaid and childcare benefits, making it almost impossible to transition from welfare to work. Since a marriage partner's income would be deducted from benefits, it was better to keep the relationship informal and not get married. AFDC needed change and improvement. It certainly got change.

Despite his rhetoric, President Reagan had only limited success in limiting "welfare," that is, the AFDC program. It took a Democratic president, who had campaigned on a promise to "end welfare as we know it," to eliminate the entitlement that had existed since the Depression. President Bill Clinton joined with a Republican Congress in 1996 to pass the Personal Responsibility and Work Opportunity Reconciliation Act (PRWORA), popularly known as "Welfare Reform," to change almost every aspect of federal and state public assistance.

The best-known and most controversial part of PRWORA rescinded the AFDC program and replaced it with Temporary Assistance for Needy Families (TANF) block grants to the states. This change converted welfare from an *entitlement* that paid cash benefits to all needy parents who met income restrictions into a combined cash benefit/work program whose benefits were contingent upon meeting work or work-preparation requirements. Open-ended federal funding to the states was replaced with block grants—fixed amounts determined by AFDC funding levels for 1994–1995 that could also be used for other purposes—thereby giving states a financial incentive to lower welfare caseloads. Most important, however, no matter how little income families had, they no longer had an entitlement to assistance. Government no longer required itself to help even destitute families.

Aside from the fixed funding (which is not indexed to inflation) through block grants, there are several major differences between TANF and AFDC. The first is "work supports." Under TANF, states now have far more discretion than under AFDC to spend funds for purposes other than cash assistance. The block grants can fund transportation, wage subsidies, pregnancy prevention programs, childcare, and state earned income tax credits to support participants in their "transition to work." For example, in an effort to "make work pay," some states now allow welfare recipients to keep more of their earnings, thus making work more attractive. States are encouraged to innovate and create new approaches. Like AFDC, TANF is a combined federal/state program. In order to qualify for full funding, states must continue to spend from their own coffers at least 75 percent of what they spent under AFDC.

Mandated work requirements are a major part of the legislation. Cash assistance is designed to be temporary, and recipients must transition "from welfare to work." States must sanction recipients who fail to meet state work requirements by reducing or eliminating their cash benefits and, sometimes, their food stamps. The federal government will reduce the block grants of states that fail to move enough recipients into jobs.

Time limits are also important signals to the states that recipients are to be moved off the rolls. In almost all instances, states are prohibited from using federal funds to give cash assistance to an individual for more than sixty months in her lifetime. States have the option of setting time limits as short as twenty-four months. Again, states are penalized through reductions in funding if appropriate numbers of people receiving cash assistance are not off the rolls soon enough. The states' freedom to individualize their programs under the broad guidelines of the legislation does not extend to modification of this basic goal: to get people off welfare (not, it must be noted, out of poverty).

Next to TANF, the most controversial provisions in the PRWORA legislation were those that sharply restricted benefits for immigrants. The 1996 legislation essentially eliminated cash assistance, food stamps, Medicaid, SSI disability, and other benefits for almost 90 percent of immigrants. Congress modified the immigrant provisions in 1997 to restore some benefits to disabled immigrants who had arrived before 1996. In May 2002 the Farm Bill reinstated food stamp benefits for adult legal immigrants who have lived in the United States for at least five years, with no minimum residency requirement for their children or the disabled. Otherwise, until they become citizens, legal immigrants (including children) arriving after 1996 have no access to government assistance—for example, SSI or Medicaid—regardless of need.

Although not well publicized, PRWORA also contained the most extensive revision of the food stamp program in twenty years. In addition to reducing funding across the board by about 3 percent, the legislation greatly restricted access to the program for adults without children, limiting them to three months of food stamps every three years. Since food stamps had previously been almost the only reliable source of additional income for these adults,[13] it was a drastic change that received little public attention, which was surprising for a program that enjoys broad public support. Most people believe that even the "undeserving poor" should have food!

Under the Supplemental Security Income program (SSI), the families of disabled children receive up to $484 per month in cash assistance. Acting on the perception that SSI payments were being given for children who were not, in fact, disabled, eligibility standards were tightened under Welfare Reform, rendering approximately 15 percent of current recipients—135,000 poor children—ineligible.[14] According to the Children's Defense Fund, more than half of all applicants are being rejected under the new criteria.

Welfare Reform changed the nature of federal support for childcare by increasing funding, consolidating programs under block grants, and allowing up to 30 percent of TANF funding to be used for childcare work support.

The provisions to improve enforcement of child support by noncustodial parents were the most extensive parts of the 1996 legislation. The goals of these reforms were to increase the determinations of paternity, locate more noncustodial parents, and improve the enforcement of child support laws. Finally, there were cutbacks to various child nutrition programs.

Evaluations of the impact of PRWORA have been tentative for four crucial reasons. First, the legislation fails to mandate a comprehensive evaluation of the program. Required state reporting under the law is remarkably minimal. This makes assessment difficult, especially given the wide latitude and encouragement the states have received to craft innovative programs. There is no longer one national program to evaluate, but more than fifty regional ones. Some states have emphasized financial incentives to work. Minnesota, for example, gives cash assistance even to families whose income leaves them well over the official poverty level and offers recipients generous benefits. It also supplements job earnings with a state earned income tax credit and provides substantial work supports, including a childcare program available to many poor working families. The aim is to encourage higher work participation rates among families on the rolls and to increase total income by mixing earnings and assistance.

Other states, like Wisconsin, have emphasized caseload reduction. Strong work supports like childcare assistance are given, but the push is simply to get people off the rolls. Approximately 25 percent of families have left the Wisconsin program because of sanctions. Former governor Tommy Thompson, now Secretary for Health and Human Services in the administration of George Bush Jr., reported that the number of people receiving cash assistance had declined 93 percent since 1987, when Wisconsin began its own welfare reforms.[15] Not surprisingly, the incomes of two-thirds of those who left the Wisconsin program remain below even the official poverty level.[16]

In some states, it is hard to know what is happening because reporting has been so minimal.

The second reason that evaluation of the program has been difficult is that an important part of the legislation is the mandated time limit that permanently prohibits states from using federal money to give cash benefits to any family head-of-household for more than sixty months in her lifetime. Because the first families only met that sixty-month limit in late 2001, there is no data on what happens to these families. Since it has already been demonstrated that sanctioned families are far less likely to find employment than families that leave the rolls for other reasons, the impact of the time limits will most likely be harsh, but this cannot yet be evaluated.

A third reason it is difficult to evaluate the impact of the 1996 legislation is that its effects are hard to separate from those linked to a number of other federal and state legislative changes designed to "make work pay." The most important of these were both federal and state earned income tax credits that effectively increase the income of the working poor and the increase in the federal minimum wage. Other such policies included expanded public health insurance for low-income children not receiving cash assistance, increased spending on childcare subsidies, and increased earned income "disregards" that allow welfare recipients to keep more of their earnings when they work while on welfare. While only the earned income tax credit and the increase in the minimum wage have had major impact on poverty, each of these policies increased to some extent the incomes of low-wage workers or provided them with other benefits.

Finally, from 1996, when the law was passed until the end of 2000, the United States economy enjoyed an uninterrupted boom of staggering proportions that increased employment, reduced poverty, and increased both state and local tax coffers. Unemployment fell to historic lows, making it easier for poor people to get jobs. Because of the hot economy, states took in more tax money, while having to deal with less poverty, than is likely to be the case in years to come. Since the amounts of the TANF block grants were based on state needs during the base period 1994–95, when we were coming out of a recession (and the need for assistance, therefore, relatively greater), the states have until now received proportionally more, in both tax revenue and block grants, per poor person than they will now that the economy is undergoing one of its periodic slowdowns. With more income and fewer recipients the states *should* be doing quite well. The real test will come in the next few years as the country experiences the effects of the current economic slide. States have already begun cutting programs because of dwindling resources and projected increases in caseloads.[17]

Since the "success" of the welfare reform legislation depends so completely on the goals one considers important, evaluation is bound to be controversial. While the extraordinary growth of the economy during the first five years of the legislation impairs any attempt at definitive evaluation, some results are nevertheless clear.

If the primary goal of welfare reform was to devolve responsibility for welfare from the federal government to the states, the PRWORA has been an unqualified success!

If the primary goal of welfare reform was "to end welfare dependence" (usually meaning to reduce welfare rolls), the legislation far exceeded anyone's expectations. Nationwide, rolls are down more than 50 percent, from 5 million families in 1994 to 2.2 million in June 2000, a remarkable change. Equally important, between 1994 and 2001 the employment rate for single mothers rose from 59 percent to 74 percent.[18] While a strong economy and work supports not included in PRWORA are certainly part of the explanation for this rise, there are good reasons to believe that the legislation played a major role as well. For example, no similar change in welfare participation or single-parent employment rates was recorded under AFDC during the economic boom of the 1980s. Since the block grants amounts are constant, this decline in caseloads has meant that states are awash in funds to use for other purposes, including work supports.

If, on the other hand, the primary goal of welfare reform had been to lift people out of poverty, matters would be far less clear. It is certainly true that the overall poverty rate has been declining steadily, from 15.1 percent in 1993 to 11.3 percent in 2000, and the poverty rate among African Americans, Hispanics, and other minorities, while still appalling, has been declining at an even more rapid pace. The level of childhood poverty is, by many measures, the lowest in a generation. The role that the welfare reform legislation has had in this decline, however, is unclear. By the middle of 2001, when the first effects of the economic slowdown were felt, the poverty rate increased again to approximately 11.8 percent, and greater increases are expected. The problem is that working parents who have left the rolls typically have low earnings, with a median wage (among those who are working) of $7.15[19] an hour and annual earnings around $8,000 to $12,000 (because most do not work full time, year-round), not enough to bring even the smallest family above the poverty level and certainly not enough to live on.

More ominous, it appears that forty percent of families that leave the rolls end up with neither job nor cash assistance. In some states, the use of sanctions—reducing or eliminating assistance for noncompliance with program rules—has accounted for a large part of those leaving welfare. Although very few states have followed sanctioned families to find out what happens to them, studies show that sanctioned families tend to have multiple barriers to employment—little education or work history, higher incidences of mental and physical illnesses and disabilities, inability to speak English, or the need to care for a disabled parent or child in the home.[20] An Urban Institute study found that among those who left TANF with three or more such barriers only

9 percent were working.[21] (Among all parents leaving welfare, approximately half are working at any given time.) A recent study in Michigan found that those who were forced from TANF because of sanctions were also more likely than those who left for other reasons to have been victims of domestic violence and to be mentally ill. In a three-city study, 93 percent of families forced from TANF because of sanctions remained in poverty.[22]

A major unanticipated and deleterious effect of welfare reform has been the steep decline in participation in both the food stamp and Medicaid programs. Prior to the legislation, a family qualifying for cash benefits was almost automatically enrolled in both Medicaid and the food stamp program. The stated intention of the 1996 law was to keep these non-cash supports in place as people moved off the welfare rolls.

These unexpected declines in food stamp and Medicaid participation appear to have a number of causes. First, income requirements in some states have kept many former AFDC recipients off Medicaid. In half the states, a working mother with two children is ineligible for Medicaid if she earns more than $9,780 a year, an amount that nonetheless leaves her family nearly $5,000 below the official poverty line.[23] In some states, the eligibility cutoff is even lower. Second, many former AFDC recipients were under the mistaken impression that they were no longer eligible for food stamps and/or Medicaid when they lost their cash benefits, and it is clear that some states did little to correct this misunderstanding. In fact, many caseworkers were under the impression that they were to de-emphasize the right to maintain access to food stamps or Medicaid. Finally, in many other cases it appears that the application and renewal processes were too difficult and time consuming for parents who were now working full time. If it takes the better part of a day or several different visits to renew one's food stamps, most employees at entry-level jobs have to make a choice between keeping their jobs and keeping the food stamps.

A study by the nonpartisan Urban Institute found that half the families that lost cash assistance also lost food stamps, although the income of the vast majority would have allowed them to continue to qualify for the program. Even more troubling, among very-low-income families (less than 50 percent of poverty level), over half no longer received food stamps.[24] Similar studies by the Center for Budget and Policy Priorities show that more than a third of the children (and more than half of the parents) of those families leaving welfare also lose Medicaid, although the vast majority still technically qualify.[25] Since both food stamps and Medicaid are in-kind benefits, neither counts when officially determining poverty. Thus while families that lose these benefits are clearly "poorer," there will be no change in the usual poverty statistics. Their substantial losses are statistically invisible.

Families that leave TANF for work become poorer in other ways, too. As everyone knows, there are expenses connected to maintaining a job, most notably childcare. While many states have attempted to provide free childcare for those leaving the rolls, available estimates are that these programs accommodate only 12 percent of the need.[26] Mothers with incomes below the poverty level spend an average of 23 percent of their income on childcare,[27] meaning that they are automatically $2,500 to $4,000 poorer, figures that won't show up in official poverty statistics either.

While the overall poverty rate is declining, those who remain poor are even poorer than before. The "poverty gap" is the amount of money that would have to be distributed to all poor families in order to bring each up to the poverty level. While the poverty rate has declined substantially since the Welfare Reform Act passed, the poverty gap for single-parent mothers who were poor worsened from $5 billion to $6.3 billion. Since there are also fewer families left below the poverty level, those that remain are consequently even poorer than before. Other statistics show that the average income of those who remain poor has been declining. All of these figures, of course, came during a period of unparalleled economic expansion that appears to be over.

Still to be felt are the effects of the five-year time limits, which began to be enforced for some families in 2001. Even more ominous is what will happen in the immediate future as the economic recession makes jobs harder to get and reduces state tax funds, while federal funding fails to expand to fill the gap.

How do we make sense of these confusing and seemingly contradictory bits of evaluation data? Many of us on the left predicted catastrophic results, with increasing poverty, state competition (a "race to the bottom") to reduce benefits to avoid becoming magnets for welfare recipients, and generalized destitution. Clearly, this has not happened—at least not yet. Why?

Three answers to this question stand out. First, the Personal Responsibility and Work Opportunity Reconciliation Act of 1996 removed the anti-work disincentives in AFDC and added significant positive incentives to work. Mothers could go to work and still keep Medicaid, mothers could get childcare *only* by going to work, and in many states mothers could continue to get TANF benefits during their first years on the job. Surprising many people, most states strengthened these positive incentives with their own funds. In that sense, TANF is a much better program than AFDC.

Second, the strong economy and constant TANF funding provided the states with much more money per recipient than under AFDC. Because of this, the effects of welfare reform have been just the opposite of what almost everyone expected: benefits became more generous. TANF money was then used to maintain (and in some cases increase) monthly benefits, but, more important, it was used in many states to create substantial work supports that made it possible for the first time for low-income single parents to move off welfare.

Finally, welfare reform has not yet met either of its primary challenges: time limits and economic recession. What will happen when women who really cannot get or hold jobs run past their sixty-month limit? We don't know. For people whose time limits have run out, states are *allowed* to continue welfare benefits in two ways. First, up to 20 percent of the state caseload may comprise families that have been on welfare past the sixty-month time limit. Second, states may use their *own* funds (as opposed to federal TANF grant funds) to provide these extended benefits. Clearly some states will choose to continue benefits past the cut-off point. Others clearly will not (since some states have already sanctioned large numbers of people and simply stopped following them). We also don't know what will happen during recession. And because evaluation takes time, the likelihood is that we will not know what has really happened until years after these changes take place.

HAS WELFARE REFORM BEEN A GOOD THING OR NOT?

In states with active work support programs, welfare reform has clearly been a force toward self-sufficiency for parents who have been able to get and keep a full-time job. Although wages have been modest (averaging $7.15 an hour) for women com-

ing off welfare, if a person took advantage of the Earned
Income Tax Credit, was able to maintain Medicaid coverage,
stayed on food stamps, was able to secure state-funded childcare, and in addition was able—through earned income disregards—to maintain a small welfare check, TANF has provided
a boost. The combination of earnings and work supports has
made low-income children and single mothers (taken as a single group) economically better off than they were under
AFDC.[28] Research shows that if income in a poor family goes
up, children do better, even if the mother has to go out to work,
so the children have benefited as well. For these families welfare reform has been a good thing.

Because states have had excess funds, considerably more
money is being spent per recipient than in AFDC. The work support programs so conspicuously absent in AFDC (childcare,
transportation, Medicaid for those working) have been the cor-
nerstone of TANF, and that has been a very good thing.

For immigrants (who essentially lost all forms of social insurance), for people who lost Medicaid, food stamps, and funded
childcare, for those living in states without active programs, and
for those who have not been able for whatever reason to get or
maintain a full-time job, welfare reform has had very different
effects. For these people, income has dropped significantly, and
the non-cash supports that helped them keep their heads above
water have disappeared. Indeed, they are drowning.

The statistics describing the "average welfare recipient" have
looked good. But these favorable numbers mask substantial subgroups of people whom society has once again abandoned.
PRWORA fails to provide for those members of our society who,
while not technically disabled, are unlikely ever to support

themselves fully in a competitive work world. People have cognitive limitations, emotional disorders, psychiatric disorders, and physical disabilities or illnesses that render them unable to work in the usual jobs. There are people whom society needs to support—either temporarily while they get back on their feet or permanently—if they are not to sink into destitution. It's not always clear who these people are, determining what is appropriate help is neither an easy nor a straightforward process. But the tools for such sophisticated evaluation do exist—cognitive and psychological testing, interviews by professionals, medical evaluation. To help the poor, however, we need to be willing to apply them in a nuanced way. We have designed our system to make sure that no "undeserving poor" get public assistance. This is the essential heartlessness and destructiveness of welfare reform. We consign hundreds of thousands of families to extreme poverty and close the door behind us. It is the old "deserving" versus "undeserving" struggle once again. We help those who can get and maintain jobs (the "deserving") while the rest are left to their own resources.

Finally, there is the unknown. In addition to time limits and economic recession, there are some states that are simply not evaluating the results of their programs. Since this process is not easy, it will be difficult for independent monitors to keep track of more than fifty state programs. We simply don't know what will happen.

Welfare reform, then, has been very good for some, very bad for others, and a very dangerous experiment in the unknown for still others.

A TATTERED SAFETY NET

So, what's left? What are the major elements of American social welfare in 2002?

In the United States, much of social welfare is actually private and employer-based, especially private health insurance and pensions. In the last twenty years the trend has been for employers either to eliminate or reduce some of these benefits. Particularly troublesome for low-wage workers is the increasing tendency of employers to hire workers part time, making them ineligible for employer-based benefits. Nevertheless, the majority of people with health insurance or pensions still get them through their jobs. Although both unemployment insurance and Workers' Compensation are legislatively mandated, they, too, are employer-based. While we usually do not think of these job benefits as part of our country's social welfare policy they are, in fact, critical aspects of it.

Probably the most important, and certainly the most overlooked, government-run anti-poverty program is the Earned Income Tax Credit (EITC). An idea backed and turned into legislation by the Republican administrations of Richard Nixon and Gerald Ford, then expanded significantly under the Democratic administration of Bill Clinton, the EITC offers low-income working people a maximum of $4,008 in yearly tax credits in order to "make work pay." The credit varies with family size and with income. For very-low-income families with two children, the credit gradually increases to its maximum when income rises to $10,000, providing an extra financial incentive to go to work. For incomes over $13,100, the tax credit gradually decreases until it phases out entirely at $32,121. It is important that these credits are "refundable," meaning that if they are more than the federal tax due, a family receives the balance as a cash refund.

The credit can have as much value as a two-dollars-per-hour raise, and studies have shown the EITC to be very effective at helping to raise people out of poverty and encouraging low-income parents to get jobs. Recent census data show that among working families, the EITC lifts substantially more children out of poverty than any other current government program or category of programs. Although there has recently been more criticism of the cost of the program, it has remained politically popular, presumably because it provides no disincentive to work. Indeed, it is only available to working people.

In July 2001, the federal child tax credit was increased from $500 to $1,000 and made partially refundable. Although the refundable credit is only available to families with incomes between $10,000 and $110,000 (and thus does not help extremely poor families at all), it will eventually be, in effect, a stipend of up to $1,000 per year per child to families with poverty-level incomes.

While Social Security benefits the poor and non-poor alike, it is an extraordinarily important and effective anti-poverty program primarily because it ensures that everyone will have some retirement income, but also because low-income workers receive a higher percentage of their lifetime earnings than do high-income workers.[29] Similarly, although Medicare is available to all elderly persons, it disproportionately benefits the poor, who would otherwise be unable to afford any care. Supplemental Security Income (SSI) is a federal income maintenance program for elderly or disabled people whose incomes fall below certain cutoffs. It supplements Social Security payments for those whose retirement income is inadequate, and it provides income for those whose mental or physical disabilities are significant enough to qualify them for the program. SSI benefits for a single person living alone are currently just over $500 a month and will therefore not raise even a single individual out of poverty. Nevertheless, benefits are pegged to inflation so that, in contrast to most public assistance programs, their real value remains constant.

Temporary Assistance for Needy Families (TANF) remains an important program for families with small children, as does Medicaid, which covers not only young families but also the disabled. What has largely been missed in the welfare debate is the fact that neither AFDC nor TANF was ever intended to make people self-reliant. Their purpose has always been to *alleviate* poverty through direct cash grants, rather than change the conditions in which the poor live. To call either program a failure because it has not raised people out of poverty is like calling the fire department a failure for not preventing a city's fires. While welfare funds are a necessary bridge to keep families from utter destitution, welfare reform recognized that those funds *must* be accompanied by other programs if they are to give families the resources to escape the "surround."

The Food Stamp program, administered through the Department of Agriculture, has generally been credited with virtually eliminating malnutrition from hunger in the United States. Before welfare reform, food stamps were available to anyone whose income was less than 130 percent of the poverty level. While the food stamp program still remains a valuable resource for poor families, PRWORA has severely limited the availability of food stamps for single adults and childless couples, who can now receive food stamps for a total of only three months during any three-year period. Food stamps have also been severely limited for immigrants. Probably as a result of these limitations, soup kitchens and food pantries around the country have reported substantial increases in demand for food since 1996.

Despite the massive cutbacks of the early 1980s, there is still some public housing (with rents proportional to income). There are also "Section 8" vouchers, in which the federal government charges recipients one-third of their income for the vouchers and then pays landlords a government-determined fair market rent. While many poor people would be eligible for housing assistance, and while the programs are very important to the people they serve, waiting lists are long (up to ten years in the District of Columbia), so the large majority of eligible people do not, in fact, benefit at all from these programs.

At the state and local level, General Assistance, that is, public relief to anyone who is poor, has largely disappeared over the past twenty years. Most state and local assistance is now in the form of social services such as child protection, shelters for the homeless, and grants to voluntary institutions to provide particular services, rather than cash grants.

This raggedy assortment of programs is especially hard on poor children. The United States separates public assistance from social insurance and then tries to distinguish between the "deserving" and "undeserving" as it parcels out benefits that no one can live on. Even in a moment of unparalleled wealth, America responds to its poor poorly, often punitively, and in many cases harshly. The system itself telegraphs an underlying message to the poor by every means possible—and increasingly since the welfare reform of the 1990s: you are at fault for your own condition and you do not deserve even what little you get. As the richest among the rich nations, the United States maintains a population of poor people of a size and in a condition that would shame any other advanced industrial country. Among those living in poverty, for all the reasons discussed in this book, African Americans are treated worst, and are largely left to fend for themselves in impoverished, run-down ghetto areas whose rebuilding is generally on no one's agenda.

There is also the generally ignored question of what happens to the fabric of society when that society refuses to care for its poorest. Welfare reform's five-year limitation on TANF benefits sends a crystal-clear message: no matter how poor you are, no matter what the external conditions causing your poverty, after five years you are on your own! It is true that the law contains some provisions allowing the states to extend benefits for a limited number of people, but there is no requirement that they do so. When the richest country in the world simply says "No more!" to its poorest, the delicate fabric that holds a society together is torn. It does not bode well for our future.

There are other options.

Five
WELFARE ELSEWHERE

We Americans have largely convinced ourselves that not only will we always have the poor with us, but also nothing can really be done about it. It's just part of the human condition, we tell ourselves, that more than 10 percent of Americans—even in the best of times—are desperately, even hopelessly poor and living in a kind of misery unimaginable to the rest of us. The idealistic hope that inspired the War on Poverty for those few short years is gone, replaced by the cynical view that any serious attempt to alleviate severe economic inequality is either doomed to failure, like the war on poverty, or another example of hopelessly utopian dreaming.

Our cynicism is unfounded. It's not as if we needed to take steps never attempted before on the face of the earth. Most of what we could do to radically improve the lives of the those most greatly in need and, indeed end poverty as we know it, has already been done and done successfully in other parts of the world. We need only take a look at the actions (which can no longer even be called experiments) of other advanced industrial countries.

The developed nations of Western Europe and Canada have taken a very different approach to social welfare. Their emphasis is on social insurance, not public assistance. There is nothing similar to Medicaid, for example, since *everyone* has access to tax-supported health care. In most of these nations, every family with children receives an allowance of some sort, so a special program directed only at needy families is less necessary. Even those programs that are specific to people living in poverty are still seen as "insurance" against the possibility of *anyone's* falling through the safety net. In the United States, the emphasis is on assistance to the needy; in most other industrialized nations the emphasis is on a social contract. In return for participating in society to the extent an individual is capable, the nation guarantees everyone a certain basic standard of living.

MAKING WELFARE WORK: A FINNISH EXAMPLE

One aspect of social insurance common to all other Western industrialized nations is universal health care. In Finland, for example, the system is a mixture of public and private medicine. (Cold-war stereotypes to the contrary, Finland's economy is capitalist, as are the economies of the other Western industrialized nations.) Physicians work thirty-seven hours a week as state employees, either in public clinics or hospitals, but are allowed to have private practices as well, which most do. Any individual may use the public clinics for a nominal fee of approximately $15[1] a year. Necessary hospitalization costs several dollars a day. Finns may also decide to use the private system, in which case the state will pay approximately two-thirds of charges for covered services. In other Western countries the mechanism for providing the coverage varies. In Canada, for example, physicians are in private practice and the state acts as a single large insurance company that physicians then bill for services. England, on the other hand, has a completely socialized system of medicine in which all physicians are state employees. In each country, however, all citizens receive basic health care as a right. In Finland, health care is also available to anyone with permanent resident status.

To American ears perhaps the strangest parts of the Finnish system are the programs of family support and home-childcare support. All families, regardless of income, receive family support allowances from the Finnish government for each of their children up to the age of seventeen. Stranger still to American minds, the *per-child* allowance increases with every additional child, in part because of government policy to encourage a higher birth rate. A family receives approximately $90 a month for a first child, but $131 a month for a third. A family with three children, for instance, would receive $330 a month in total child support payments.

A single mother receives an additional $44 a month per child. A single mother is also guaranteed at least $107 a month in child support from the child's father. Unlike in the United States, where few poor single parents receive child support, in Finland the government guarantees payment by taking responsibility for collecting child support payments and supplying the mother any unpaid balance if the state is for any reason unable to collect from the father.[2]

In addition to receiving basic child support, one of the parents (or the single parent) of pre-school-age children can choose to stay home to provide childcare and receives a $250-per-month base "salary." The stay-at-home caregiver receives an additional $85 a month for each child up to the age of four and $50 a month for each older child. Single parents who choose to stay home (and thus have no other income) or poor two-parent families receive an additional payment of up to $170 a month, depending on family size and income.[3]

A single parent of two small children can, therefore, choose to "work at home" and receive a basic income of over $12,000 a year, in a country where a poverty level income for that person is

$15,000.[4] Additional assistance to pay rent, which is also available, would bring the income well above the poverty level.

For parents who choose to return to work, the state provides childcare for a charge of $200 a month for the first child, $200 a month for the second child, and $40 a month for each additional child. This charge is reduced for low-income families and is free for families with an income less than $12,000 a year.

While the numbers work out differently elsewhere, family support in other industrialized countries is similarly generous. In Finland, France, Sweden, and several other countries in Europe, maternity allowances pay an amount almost equal to regular salaries for up to a year. In fact, the United States is the only industrialized country that does not have universal preschool, family assistance, and parental leave programs.

Unemployment insurance benefits are approximately half of one's previous salary, which is about the same amount as in the United States, but almost everyone who loses a job receives it (in the United States less than half do), and an unemployed worker can receive those benefits for up to two years, compared to six months in the United States.

All Finns, regardless of income, are also eligible for allowances for almost any kind of adult education, be it university classes, vocational or job training, continuing job-related education, or retraining for a new profession. In addition, tuition is free at all Finnish schools for everyone. Students (including full-time adult students) also receive a living support of $260 a month as well as rent support, which is two-thirds of monthly rent up to a maximum of $150 a month.

Retirement benefits are handled much as in the United States, with a combination of private retirement funds through employers and state-financed social security benefits which would be considered generous by American standards.

In addition to these benefits, available to everyone regardless of income, there are two programs specifically designed for the economically needy. The first is rent assistance, which is available at up to 80 percent of monthly rent, depending on one's income and the cost of rent. Renters can choose housing wherever they can find it, preventing the kind of economic ghettoization that is common in the United States. The names of those receiving such assistance are confidential, which avoids any stigma.

Finally, there is a catchall benefit that social workers can authorize for people who still fall through the cracks. The amount one should need to live on is determined by a schedule that factors in family size, cost of living in the area, and any special needs.[5] If all of one's income, including salaries, allowances and supports, is less than the determined amount, the social worker may, on a case-by-case basis, authorize an extra allowance to bring one up to the predetermined level, which is approximately the poverty level. A single mother with two children who rents an apartment for $600 a month, for example, is considered to need an amount almost identical to our poverty level of $15,590 for a family of three. Unlike the other entitlements, these catchall allowances are administered individually by assigned social workers to make sure that funds are being used appropriately.[6] If other special needs do develop, one can return to the social worker and apply for additional assistance.

When we, as Americans, look at such a social welfare system, invariably our first response is, "With benefits like that, who would want to go to work?" We wonder how many people are simply playing the system. When I tried to voice that concern in an interview with a Finnish social worker, she at first didn't even grasp what I was getting at. She finally responded that in her city of sixty thousand people, a study had indicated that approximately one hundred people were receiving benefits who "should have been working." She went on to say, however, that the agency had just done a more in-depth study of these one hundred individuals. Extensive medical and psychological testing had determined that approximately half had subtle disabilities that actually did prevent them from working. In that particular city, then, the agency believed that less than one person in a thousand was abusing the system. Although no similar systematic nationwide study has been done, a high-level administrator in Helsinki agreed that such abuse was rare.

Because virtually all Finns belong to the same racial and cultural group, racial segregation is not an issue in Finland, nor is there much economic segregation. Rich and poor live in the same neighborhoods; their children go to the same schools. As a consequence, the disparity in services like education, police protection, or trash pickup provided to rich and poor, so prominent in the United States, is largely absent.

The result of this system is that Finland has little poverty as we in the United States would define it. There is certainly inequality, but low-income people's incomes are generally not allowed to fall below our poverty levels. Even the most needy, then, would not be "poor" by our definition.

There is, of course, a cost to such a way of organizing society. In the United States, average Federal and local taxation rates— exclusive of social security payroll taxes—are about 21 percent of income, and many Americans consider these rates high. Taxation rates in Finland and other Western nations range from 40 percent to 50 percent of income, although not all of the difference is due to social insurance programs.

A commonly expressed objection is that America's problems are different from Finland's. Finland is a small country. The population is much more homogeneous and therefore people tend to identify with one another. The overwhelming issue of segregation (and the legacy of slavery) does not exist. Immigration is only a minor issue. Furthermore, it is pointed out that European countries themselves have recently been scaling down their own social programs because of the expense. But the objections are not as persuasive as they first appear.

Finland is indeed a small country, but much larger countries like Germany and France have programs that provide similar social insurance for the needs of children, as well as for illness, maternity, retirement, and unemployment. While there is certainly poverty in these countries, it does not reach the level of destitution familiar to us here, and children tend to be the best-off demographic group, not the poorest, as in the United States. Why should size alone constrain the development of an adequate safety net, especially if federal funding and standards are combined with local administration?

It is true that the other developed countries are not burdened by America's history of racism and that some, like Finland, are much more homogeneous than we are. Because our population is highly segregated by race and class, the affluent do not have the poor as friends or even personal acquaintances, so the poor tend to remain "the other," believed to be responsible for their own destitution. It is, therefore, difficult to mobilize political support for social insurance. But this explains only America's political reluctance to embrace an adequate social safety net. It is not an argument against social insurance in itself. Furthermore, not all developed countries are as homogeneous as Finland. Canada, Germany, and England all contain diverse populations yet manage to prevent destitution far better than the United States does.

While some European countries have limited their social programs in recent years, these cutbacks have been overemphasized in the American press. After the breakup of the Soviet Union, Finland experienced several years of severe recession as commerce with its major trading partner all but collapsed and the official unemployment rate reached 22 percent. Despite this extraordinary stress on the safety net, however, there were no significant reductions in benefits. Over the past ten years, I have several times read in the American press allusions to cutbacks in Finland's social insurance. As I have asked Finns about each "cutback," however, either no one knew anything about it or the cutback was a minor tweaking of the system. The European safety nets remain largely intact.

There are several take-home lessons for Americans here:

○ It is possible to create a national social insurance program that does not allow anyone's income to fall below a level considered necessary to live decently. So defined, poverty is not an inescapable fact of human nature, political science, or even a capitalist economy.

○ Creating such a system is expensive. It requires significantly higher levels of taxation than Americans have been willing to allow.

○ There is nothing intrinsic in this kind of social insurance that leads to lack of motivation or laziness. Given the proper support, most people will use the program appropriately. It is important to recognize, however, that the enormous physical and psychic damage already done to too many poor people in our country would demand much more intensive and expensive support for the first generation or two.

How, then, might we build such a system in the United States?

Six

ENDING POVERTY AS WE KNOW IT

AS LONG AS THERE ARE GHETTOS...

In eradicating urban poverty in the United States, by far the most important policy change would be a strong commitment to the goal of desegregation, both racial and economic. As long as there are ghettos, Jonathan Kozol has written, there will be ghetto desperation. If one puts all of the poorest people together in one area, removes the jobs, decimates social networks, and thus causes the myriad problems that result, generational despair is simply inevitable.

In his book *Return Flight*, Robert Lupton describes the concept of "re-neighboring" and his experience in moving his own family and other affluent people into poor urban neighborhoods. The advantages of living in a diverse, lively city neighborhood are becoming attractive to some. By bringing their skills and education to a neighborhood, moving in their own families, encouraging the development of low-income housing, helping neighbors to buy their homes or apartments so that gentrification will not drive them out, and creating new living spaces, small groups of people have revitalized neighborhoods without forcing residents out and completely gentrifying the areas. While this is, I think, unlikely to become a mass movement, Lupton's experiment indicates that there are ways of revitalizing neighborhoods without removing the poor.

A more common opportunity for cities is the process of gentrification that often occurs. Neighborhoods change. For one reason or another—dissatisfaction with commuting, desire to live in a city once children are grown, the cost of owning or renting—affluent people begin moving into less affluent neighborhoods. Developers buy up old properties and build new luxury apartments. The usual story is that the poor are pushed out to other, worse neighborhoods. That doesn't have to happen, however. City governments can steer the gentrification process onto another track that maintains the area's affordable housing. The property tax structure can be changed so that low-income homeowners aren't forced out by climbing tax assessments. Low-interest loans can be made available to tenants to purchase their buildings and create affordable housing. Tax incentives and permit requirements can induce developers to create a certain number of low-income units in their new buildings. Vibrant, diverse neighborhoods *can* be built.

On a potentially much larger scale, there have been some interesting experiments that bring indigent people into affluent neighborhoods. The specter of "the poor" moving into "our" world is threatening to most middle- and upper-class Americans. We fear that the problems of the inner city will accompany them. One fascinating study, conducted over the last twenty-five years, has been the Gautreaux Project in Chicago. Its profound implications have not, however, been generally recognized. Chicago public housing has always been highly segregated. As part of the settlement of a federal civil rights suit in the 1970s, the city of Chicago agreed to fund a study of what happened to approximately five thousand families from a public housing project that was being razed. The tenants were, for all practical purposes, randomly assigned to two groups. Both groups were offered federal housing vouchers that could be used anywhere a landlord would accept them. Families in the "inner-city group" were offered the usual social service agency help in finding housing in another inner-city area. Families in the "suburban group," however, were given the opportunity to move into affluent, usually white, neighborhoods in the suburbs. Other than locating landlords who would accept the housing vouchers, neither group was given any special help. These two groups were then followed closely and have been statistically compared over the last twenty-five years.

To oversimplify, the lives of the mothers in the suburban group were not startlingly different from those of the mothers in the inner-city group. Though they certainly fared better in employment, income, and independence of welfare, the differences were not great. Interestingly, though, neither group of mothers felt more socially isolated than the other, which is to say that the poor, black mothers in the white, middle-class neighborhoods felt no more socially isolated than their counterparts in the city. It was not that the suburban mothers did not often feel isolated; they did. But so did the inner-city mothers, who often felt forced to choose self-isolation as a way of protecting their children from the dangers of the ghetto.

It was in the lives of the children as they grew that the important differences were noted. As might be expected, the several years immediately following their transfer to more advanced suburban schools proved trying for children from the inner city. They had much to catch up on—in many cases years of work—because their previous schools had simply not been teaching at the same level. After three or four years, however, their performances improved markedly. They began to do as well compared to their suburban peers as their inner-city counterparts were doing compared to their inner-city peers. To express it another way, if black inner-city kids had gotten A's in the inner-city, they were now making A's in the suburbs; those with B's in the inner-city had B's in the suburbs, and so on. The children had "jumped the track" from ghetto educational standards to suburban educational standards.

Some of these children have now been followed for over twenty years, and the differences between the two groups continue to be astonishing. Far more children in the suburban group graduated from high school, ten times as many matriculated into four-year colleges, and, of those that did, there were proportionately fewer college dropouts. As these children now move into adulthood, similar differences are being found in their employment histories and income levels. While their roads through the suburbs were sometimes bumpy, and while not everyone succeeded, a high percentage of these former ghetto kids were moving out. For them, the cycle of generational poverty had been broken.

There are several conditions in the study that should be noted. First, only one or two families were moved into any particular suburban neighborhood. This was an important condition because it did not allow the children—especially the adolescents—to congregate and maintain a ghetto subculture in their new neighborhood or school. Children were essentially forced to integrate themselves into a suburban culture and leave their ghetto problems behind.

Second, their new neighbors knew nothing of their histories unless the new families chose to tell them. Neighbors were therefore allowed to form their own opinions of the newcomers without the prejudices that "the ghetto" immediately conjures.

Third, these black families were often integrated into white neighborhoods despite a considerable reluctance on the part of the black mothers. No one was forced to take the housing offered by the study, of course, but the very few who chose not to take housing offered to them were dropped from the study and had to move into the usual queues for inner-city housing. Since most African Americans understandably prefer to live in neighborhoods with something closer to a fifty-fifty racial mix, presumably most of these black families would have chosen to move into middle-class black or more integrated neighborhoods. In all probability, their children would have done just as well or better in affluent black neighborhoods, but this has not been tested.

These results must challenge those of us who blame individuals or their families for the frequent failures of the inner city. Take the families out of the inner city, the Gautreaux Project strongly suggests, and they will do as well as any ordinary range of families might. The Gautreaux Project is now being replicated in five cities across the United States in a U.S. Department of Housing and Urban Development (HUD) program called Moving to Opportunity. Since the participants only finished moving into their new homes in 1999, no experimental results are yet available. Affluent communities have in some cases reacted negatively to such projects, however, creating significant obstacles to the establishment of similar programs elsewhere. Public protest at a site chosen by HUD in Baltimore led Congress to eliminate funding for a planned expansion of the program. A similar non-HUD program in Fairfax, Virginia, a suburb of Washington, D.C., was canceled when neighbors objected to moving *one* low-income family into their affluent neighborhood.

MENDING THE SAFETY NET

In the absence of real desegregation, the task of eliminating American poverty will certainly be very difficult. It would be possible, however, to design a social insurance system that would lift the income of most poor Americans above the poverty level. The following is a proposal that, I think, could be accepted by a majority of Americans. Since it involves only one new program (favored in reliable polls by a large majority of Americans[1]) and an expansion of three currently existing ones, the proposal seems politically feasible.

First, the new program: universal health coverage. People cannot move out of poverty unless health care is provided to all Americans. Health insurance in the United States is currently largely employer-based, although fewer and fewer employers now offer it and still fewer offer fully paid family coverage. Most low-wage employers do not provide health insurance, and those that do often require unaffordable co-payments. On their own, low-income, working-class, and even middle-class people simply cannot afford family health care premiums that average more than $7,000 a year. With one out of six Americans currently uninsured and the trend away from employer-sponsored coverage, the only reasonable option seems to be some form of national health insurance. Congressman James McDermott, a physician from the state of Washington, has repeatedly introduced a proposal in the House of Representatives for a "single-payer plan" that would provide universal coverage to all Americans without increasing total health care costs for the country. Sixty to eighty members of the House have usually signed on to this bill.[2]

Like the Canadian system mentioned in the previous chapter, a single-payer plan would make the United States government into the sole "insurance company" to offer health care. Regardless of what one thinks of it in other areas, the federal government handles insurance very efficiently and cheaply. Social

Security operates with an administrative overhead of less than 3 percent compared to more than 25 percent for combined overhead and profit at private insurance companies. Doctors would remain in private practice and still bill the "insurance company," but there would be only one company to bill, the government. The plan would be administered on the state or regional level, and fee-for-service rates would be negotiated between state governments and physician representatives every year.

Such a shift would have a powerful impact on the insurance industry, and that has, of course, created strong political opposition to such a plan. There would certainly be some negative effect on the economy as private industry lost jobs that were only partially offset by new government hiring, but the increased efficiency and universal coverage would certainly be worth it.[3]

The administrative savings from such a plan would be enormous. Not only would government overhead be far less than private insurance company overhead, but administrative costs would also be less for doctors and hospitals. The current Byzantine system of private insurance—in which different policies exclude different conditions from coverage and pay varying amounts for conditions they do cover—is an expensive bureaucratic nightmare for health-care providers. In separate studies the Congressional Budget Office and the Office of Management and Budget demonstrated that the administrative savings of a single-payer plan would be enough to provide comprehensive health coverage for all of the uninsured in the country. In other words, we could give everyone access to comprehensive health care for the same total cost that now leaves over 43 million people uninsured![4]

When polled, Americans overwhelmingly favor such a plan. Typical is a *USA Today*/Harris poll from November 23, 1998, in which 77 percent of the general public and 53 percent of employers agree that "government should provide quality medical care to all adults." As the *Wall Street Journal* indicated in a 1998 article, two-thirds of Americans said they believe that "the government [should] guarantee everyone the best and most advanced health care that technology can supply."[5] Even when it was suggested that such coverage might raise taxes by $2,000 a year (probably an overly high estimate), almost half were still supporters of the plan. "The fact that almost half of the public is willing to pay $2,000 extra to guarantee access to others is striking," noted the *Journal*.[6]

So much for a much-needed new program. What of older programs already in place? First, the Earned Income Tax Credit, a well-accepted, successful program could be expanded so that no person working more than, say, thirty hours a week would earn less than the poverty level for his or her family. There are now millions of poor people who have a full-time worker in the family. With an expanded EITC, none of these families would be poor. Some state and even local governments have created their own earned income tax credit that is supplementary to the federal EITC. A further provision could offer an extra credit to parents of small children, making childcare more affordable. The coordination and expansion of these programs would bring all working people and their families out of poverty.

Second, unemployment insurance could be expanded so that employees who are laid off receive income that keeps them above the poverty level. Several administrative changes in the program would be necessary. Benefits for low-income workers would have to be supplemented to provide at least a poverty-level income to those out of work. Currently, unemployed people receive less than half of their previous income. Low-wage earners, of course, cannot live on half of already abysmally low incomes, so they would need significant supplements. This could be done through the tax code (even as part of the EITC), so that wage earners with larger families received adequate income. In addition, the benefit period would need to be extended so that workers could continue to receive benefits until they find work. People who refused appropriate work offered by employment services could have their benefits temporarily reduced. Finally, the program would need to be expanded so that all people who leave work are covered. Currently only 40 percent of unemployed workers receive any unemployment payments at all. The expansion of this program would mean that no person able and willing to work would remain in poverty.

Third, the government Supplemental Security Insurance (SSI) program, which provides disability benefits to those permanently disabled, and Workers' Compensation, which provides benefits to workers who are injured on the job, must be carefully expanded in several ways. Eligibility must be extended so that between the two programs everyone who really cannot work, for whatever reason, qualifies. Currently, for example, people who are temporarily disabled due to injuries incurred off the job receive no benefits from either program. Worse, even people who are clearly permanently disabled may not receive disability determinations. Causes such as disabling back pain (often impossible for the claimant to "prove"), mental conditions that do not meet certain criteria, disability due to addiction, and many other disabling conditions do not, in practice, make the claimant eligible. As a physician, I sometimes struggled for years to get examiners at SSI to understand that one or another of my patients was, indeed, disabled.

Here again our preoccupation with the "undeserving poor"

makes it harder for us to imagine solutions. Political attitudes and budget appropriations ensure that regulations are designed to weed out every single person who might be malingering. Informal agency attitudes, even the personal attitudes of the examiners, make the process stricter yet. But in practice it is not possible to screen out *all* those who should not qualify without excluding many who should. Of course, it is important to make sure that unemployment and disability insurances are used appropriately. But because we emphasize so strongly the exclusion of those who might not need it, too many of those with legitimate need fall through the cracks. The level of coverage under Workers' Compensation and SSI must be increased at least to the poverty level.

The total cost of these changes would not be prohibitive. The cost of universal health care would necessitate an increase in taxes, but that would be offset by the elimination of insurance premiums paid by those employers who currently provide coverage, the elimination of premiums paid by individuals for their own coverage, and the folding of Medicaid and Medicare into the new program. In addition, because coverage for medical expenses is a large part of the cost of premiums for car insurance, liability insurance, Workers' Compensation premiums, and other similar insurances, these costs would all decrease significantly if all medical bills were paid through national health insurance.

The exact cost of the other three programs is not known, although it would not require more than a relatively small (certainly less than 5 percent) increase in federal expenditures. In 1999, the total "poverty gap" (the amount of money required to raise all the incomes to the poverty line) was $65 billion.[7] By contrast, yearly Social Security income alone is approximately $500 billion. The tax deduction that homeowners are allowed to take for the interest they pay on their mortgages (really an income transfer program to the middle class!) costs the United States treasury $63.2 billion a year.[8] Compare all of this to the $1.3 trillion tax-cut of 2001, and the amounts look manageable, indeed.

Although the *political* likelihood of enacting the above programs is at present small, we should not confuse the issue by saying that we have "tried everything" to eliminate poverty or that "the government can't solve the problem of poverty." The government—that is, the American people acting together—*can* solve the problem of poverty, and it would be neither an enormously expensive nor utopian project. The problem has been that we have not been willing to consider it.

Would the above programs simply make it too easy for people to sit back and let the government take care of them? The evidence suggests not. The backbone of the above programs is the expansion of the EITC, which has consistently been shown to encourage work.[9]

AND JUSTICE FOR ALL

Even if we lift people out of poverty, of course, much of the damage that has already been done by generations of impoverishment and oppression remains and there will be much left to do. Inner-city schools will still have to be radically improved and vocational training provided for the millions who do not have the skills to enter the job market of the twenty-first century. Urban neighborhoods must be rebuilt and closer political and economic ties established between suburbs and the cities. Social services must be provided to the current victims of inner-city poverty—especially the children—to overcome some of the emotional damage already inflicted.

The details of welfare policy and governmental programs

must not be allowed to obfuscate the central truth. The larger American society, through its structures and programs, built the black urban ghettos and then decimated them; it is the responsibility of those of us who benefit from the structures and programs of our society to undo the damage. The causes of ghetto poverty do not lie in the individual behavior of inner-city African Americans, but lie primarily in forces outside their control. It is up to them to do what they humanly can; it is up to the rest of society to change existing programs and create new ones to allow *everyone* to enjoy a decent standard of living.

Justice demands that the conditions in our inner cities be changed. The current response to the problems of poverty is mostly to add police, increase prison sentences, and throw up our hands, insisting, "There's nothing more we can do." It's a response that does not match our stated values.

I have worked in the inner city for almost two decades. The poverty I see is not intractable, nor are its causes mysterious. Our social welfare programs tend to work about as well as they are designed to. We must not allow ourselves to use their failure as a rationalization that relieves us of our responsibility to our fellow citizens. The black urban ghetto exists because of concrete historical events and our failure to respond appropriately to those events. This inaction is not worthy of the American people, who are, at a personal level, eager to eradicate injustice and willing to give of their resources to do so. We must not let the poverty of the ghetto stand. Fortunately, it's not too late. We know what to do, and we have the ability and the resources to do it. It's past time that we remove this stain upon our American democracy.

Acknowledgments

Every book is the work of many people, even if only one is designated as "author," and I am grateful for all those who participated in the creation and evolution of this book. The manuscript is anchored in eighteen years of experience at Columbia Road Health Services, Community of Hope Health Services, Christ House, and Joseph's House in Washington, D.C. The staff and clients in those institutions pricked my conscience and my interest and first pushed me into questioning the origins of inner-city poverty. The Servant Leadership School of the Church of the Saviour several times gave me the opportunity to teach the course that is the origin of much of the material here. I am indebted to the students in those classes for helping me inquire more deeply and think more systematically about the inner city. Unknowingly, they reviewed the initial manuscripts and helped develop them.

Gordon Cosby first suggested that I take the content of the course and turn it into a pamphlet, which he encouraged the Servant Leadership School to publish. David Wade illustrated that early edition.

Tom Engelhardt, my editor and good friend of many years, suggested expanding the pamphlet into a book, and he connected me with Dan Simon at Seven Stories Press.

Very little in this book is original work. I have depended heavily on a rich literature. I have cited references to the direct quotations and to many of the statistics I've used from this literature, but it would be impossible to cite references to all of the ideas I've absorbed without a blizzard of endnotes. I hope that this book will be a starting point for those interested in exploring the subject further; the partial annotated bibliography at the book's end will, I hope, be helpful.

I want to offer particular thanks to various scholars and journalists for their groundbreaking or insightful studies of urban poverty. Historian Michael B. Katz, in his extensive writings, has built a framework for organizing the work of scholars in sociology, psychology, political science, and other fields. Sociologist William Julius Wilson has combined his own research with a deep understanding of the issues of poverty in a series of original books over the past twenty years. Sociologists Douglas Massey and Nancy Denton have made a powerful and convincing argument that segregation itself is the single most important cause of black urban poverty. Economist Rebecca Blank has organized a maze of statistics so clearly that causes become obvious. Writer and educator Jonathan Kozol has written passionately about his many journeys into the world of the poor, offering stories that give statistics a soul. Journalist William Finnegan and the team of journalist David Simon and sociologist Edward Burns have offered powerful narratives of individuals who must somehow live among the forces explored here. Scholars at the Center for Budget and Policy Priorities and the Children's Defense Fund have posted invaluable information to their respective Web sites. I am grateful to all of these authors for their contributions.

Many people have read and commented on the manuscript or portions of it. My wife, Marja Hilfiker; Dave and Kathy Neely;

Lois Wagner; my sister Lois Kanter; Michael Katz; and students in my class at the Servant Leadership School have all participated in the birthing of the final manuscript.

I am always amazed at how much my editor, Tom Engelhardt, improves what I send him. He is truly a coauthor, seeing what it is that I'm trying to say and pointing out ways of saying it better, suggesting further avenues to explore, asking embarrassing questions about just how I concluded such and so, and tweaking my English so that the meaning is clear. I am grateful for his work with me and for his friendship.

Finally, Dan Simon at Seven Stories Press agreed to publish the expanded manuscript, reread it, and made numerous helpful suggestions for improvement.

Without these teachers, friends, and colleagues there would be no book. I am grateful.

Annotated Bibliography

The following is not an exhaustive bibliography on inner-city poverty but a descriptive listing of the books and some Web sites that I have found most helpful.

BLANK, REBECCA. *It Takes a Nation.* Princeton University Press, Princeton, N.J., 1997. Blank, an economist who worked in the first Bush administration, offers copious statistics integrated into the text of her book, and the statistics speak volumes about the underlying causes of poverty. The book offers a good run-down of current government programs, making helpful distinctions about what local, state, and federal governments can do best and most efficiently. She argues that government programs have been far more successful than is generally appreciated. She makes it clear that poverty is, at heart, a political problem and only secondarily a social or economic one.

BROWN, MICHAEL K. *Race, Money, and the American Welfare State.* Cornell University Press, Ithaca, N.Y., 1999. An overly technical look at the truncated development of the welfare state in America. Emphasizing especially Roosevelt's New Deal and Johnson's Great Society, Brown argues that the intersection of political and fiscal conservatism and racial discrimination has created a welfare state doomed to failure, while also stigmatizing the poor through too many programs that are "means-tested" (just for the poor). He argues that only a universal welfare state (where everyone receives benefits, as in our Social Security or Unemployment Insurance programs) can succeed without stigmatization.

CANADA, GEOFFREY. *Fist, Stick, Knife, Gun: A Personal History of Violence in America.* Beacon Press, Boston, 1996. An autobiographical account by a leader in the African American community of growing up in the ghetto of the South Bronx and how the nature of inner-city violence changed significantly when easily available guns and automatic weapons replaced the fists, sticks, and knives.

COPELAND, WARREN R. *And the Poor Get Welfare: The Ethics of Poverty in the U.S.* Abingdon Press, Nashville, 1994. Copeland, a theologian who wants to develop a Christian basis on which to approach welfare, reviews the approaches to poverty of four authors, two conservatives (Charles Murray and Lawrence Mean) and two liberals (Lisbeth Schorr and Francis Fox Piven). His exploration of the philosophies and theologies behind their approaches to poverty is clear and concise, helping one understand how people can look at the same problem yet propose such vastly different solutions.

CURRIE, ELLIOTT. *Crime and Punishment in America.* Henry Holt and Company, New York, 1998. Currie, a criminologist, lays out the six-fold expansion of the American prison system in the last two decades. He explores in some detail what we can and can't expect from prisons and concludes that the current policy of incarcerating so many will only worsen our problems. He offers concrete solutions for change.

EDELMAN, PETER. *Searching for America's Heart: RFK and the Renewal of Hope.* Houghton Mifflin Company, Boston, 2001. When President Clinton decided to sign the Welfare Reform bill of 1996, Edelman, then assistant secretary for planning and evaluation in the Department of Health and Human Services and a personal friend of the President, resigned from the administration in protest. Edelman, a lawyer who began his political career working for Robert Kennedy, accompanied him on a 1967 trip through poverty-stricken rural Mississippi that strongly influenced Kennedy's politics. Half of this book is a first-person narrative of his work with Kennedy, focusing on Kennedy's evolving insights into poverty. The second half explores what those insights might still have to offer us as we struggle to deal with poverty after welfare reform.

EDIN, KATHRYN AND LEIN, LAURA. *Making Ends Meet: How Single Mothers Survive Welfare and Low-Wage Work.* Russell Sage Foundation, New York, 1997. A sociologist and anthropologist extensively interview 379 single mothers—both those with low-wage jobs and those on AFDC—in four cities and offer us an antidote to many stereotypes of poor single-parent women. Collecting information about spending habits, additional sources of income, and other details of their lives, the authors document that virtually all the women need to receive more outside income and that welfare mothers are just as good at managing their money as working mothers.

EHRENREICH, BARBARA. *Nickel and Dimed: On (Not) Getting by in America.* Metropolitan Books, New York, 2001. A vivid first-person account by a well-known, middle-aged author who tries to live for several months as a woman leaving welfare might. In three different locales around the country, she moves in, tries to find jobs without using her skills as a writer, and lives for a month, hoping to earn enough to pay the next month's rent. Her stories give a strong sense of how difficult the lives of the working poor are.

FINNEGAN, WILLIAM. *Cold New World: Growing Up in Harder Country.* Random House, New York, 1999. A writer for *The New Yorker*, Finnegan spent many months at each of four locations: New Haven, Connecticut; San Augustine County, Texas; the Yakima Valley in Washington state; and Los Angeles, California. He writes about the lives of poor and working-class young people in each place. His portrayal of poverty is compassionate without being sentimental, and detailed without being harsh.

FOLSOM, FRANKLIN. *American Before Welfare.* New York University Press, New York, 1996. A somewhat overlong narrative about American approaches to poverty before the current era, written by a man who was part of the labor struggle during the 1930s and thus has a radical labor perspective. It takes apart the conservative criticism that America used to take care of its poor very well primarily through individual effort and voluntary associations.

FRANK, ROBERT H. AND COOK, PHILIP J. *The Winner-Take-All Society: Why the Few at the Top Get So Much More Than the Rest of Us.* Penguin Books, New York, 1985. This book is not about poverty at all. Frank and Cook, academic economists, offer some tantalizing new perceptions of how our economy works and make strong arguments for a return to steeply progressive tax rates. Their argument is that, given recent changes in communications and mechanization, many sectors of the economy reward the top few people far more than those just below them, even though differences in skill levels are minimal. They argue for a steeply progressive tax not just to fund needed programs, but to bring the market back into some semblance of order.

HACKER, ANDREW. *Two Nations: Black and White, Separate, Hostile, Unequal.* Ballantine Books, New York, 1995. Primarily a look at racism in the United States, it provides a great deal of help to whites trying to understand racism. Its statistical material tends to be much better than its rhetoric, and there is much here that helps in understanding poverty.

ISSERMAN, MAURICE AND KAZIN, MICHAEL. *America Divided: The Civil War of the 1960s.* Oxford University Press, New York, 2000. Primarily a history of America in the 1960s, but with two good chapters on the War on Poverty, its theory, inception, and dismantling.

KATZ, MICHAEL B.: The foremost historian of American poverty and welfare. His books are required reading for anyone studying the subject:

In the Shadow of the Poorhouse: A Social History of Welfare in America. Revised and updated tenth anniversary edition, Basic Books, New York, 1997. A long but interesting history of poverty and welfare in the United States. It is probably the single most helpful source on the history of poverty. In writing this text, I relied heavily on Katz's ideas and structure presented here.

The Undeserving Poor. Random House, New York, 1990. Explores the long history of our attempt to separate the "deserving" from the "undeserving" poor. Our political willingness to help poor people is deeply grounded in our moral judgment of how we believe they came to be poor. Katz reviews the intellectual impact on the poverty debate of a number of influential thinkers and explores some critical notions in that debate, particularly about "the culture of poverty" and "the underclass."

Improving Poor People: The Welfare State, the "Underclass," and Urban Schools as History. Princeton University Press, Princeton, N.J., 1995. An excellent summary of some of Katz's other works, this is a series of three lengthy review articles by Katz on the welfare state, the underclass, and urban schools, along with three case histories of poverty, with commentary. Katz makes the point that that the primary approach to poverty in the United States has always been based on the thesis that if we could improve poor people themselves, poverty would go away. One difficulty with this book is that it is a summary, so some of Katz's statements— quite thoroughly researched and explored in earlier books—can seem here more like unsubstantiated opinion.

The Price of Citizenship: Redefining the American Welfare State. Metropolitan Books, New York, 2001. A close look at the history of welfare since the Family Support Act of 1988, which was in many ways the beginning of contemporary American welfare reform. Katz suggests that the deserving/undeserving dichotomy has spread into other areas of welfare such as unemployment insurance, retirement benefits, and disability insurance, all of which have become less reliable sources of support in the last decades. His ultimate question concerns the price of citizenship: how "deserving" must I be in order to qualify for the social insurance that citizenship in a wealthy state might confer?

KOZOL, JONATHAN: an educator, storyteller and author who has written eloquently, sensitively, and prolifically about poverty, usually from the point of view of the poor children he has met in his research. Although Kozol doesn't flinch from analysis and critique, each of his books is a first-person account of his own immersion into the world he visits, full of the stories of actual people, so there is an immediacy and a power in his work missing from most books analyzing and critiquing poverty and the policies that surround it.

Rachel and Her Children: Homeless Families in America. Fawcett Columbine, New York, 1989. Kozol spends time in the family shelter system of New York City. A powerful element in this book is his first-person look at the indignities of being on welfare and how difficult the system is to traverse.

Savage Inequalities: Children in America's Schools. Perennial, New York, 1992. Kozol is a muckraker of the highest caliber. This book explores the plight of inner-city schools in scathing detail.

Amazing Grace. Perennial, New York, 1996. Kozol spends months in the South Bronx, one of the poorest communities in the United States, and tells about the children he meets. He also offers the emotionally powerful, well-reasoned argument that few people would be able to escape the ravages of the inner-city ghetto and that our only option is to dismantle it.

LIEBOW, ELLIOT: Liebow was an academic sociologist. However, at the beginning and end of his academic career (he died in 1994) he did some case-study sociology, spending months in one location and writing about what he saw.

Tally's Corner. Little, Brown, Boston, 1967. A classic book on poverty, this is a study of men who hung out on a particular street corner in a Washington, D.C., inner-city area (reportedly two blocks from my former clinic). Liebow just hung around with the men and let them tell their own stories. It's a simple, short book that documents how easy it is to lose initiative after hanging out on the corner for a while.

Tell Them Who I Am: The Lives of Homeless Women. Penguin Books, New York, 1995. Liebow was working at the National Institutes of Health when he found out that he had an incurable cancer but had some time to live. He quit his job and began volunteering at a shelter and a soup kitchen in suburban Maryland just outside of Washington, D.C. Based on those experiences, this book, in a way familiar from *Tally's Corner*, lets homeless women tell their own stories and look at their own lives.

LUPTON, ROBERT D. *Return Flight: Community Development through Reneighboring Our Cities.* FCS Urban Ministries, Atlanta, 1997. A brief account of the author's move to inner-city Atlanta to establish a neighborhood integrated both racially and economically. Ghetto communities need not only outside investment but also the physical presence of the investors.

MASSEY, DOUGLAS S. AND DENTON, NANCY A. *American*

Apartheid: Segregation and the Making of the Underclass. Harvard University Press, Cambridge, Mass., 1994. The authors are sociologists who explore the history of segregation, especially northern urban segregation. They make a compelling argument that without segregation there would be no ghetto, and black and white rates of poverty would not be so dissimilar. They are convinced—and convincing—that we will never end urban poverty without dismantling the ghetto. Statistics are impressively marshaled to support their argument persuasively.

NEWMAN, KATHERINE S. *No Shame in My Game.* Vintage Books, New York, 2000. An excellent look at a crucial recent change in the face of poverty, the increasing numbers of poor people who are working full time or almost full time, yet cannot pull their families out of poverty.

PARENTI, CHRISTIAN. *Lockdown America: Police and Prisons in the Age of Crisis.* Verso, New York, 2000. This is an especially frightening book about the prison system. Parenti offers insight into the prison population explosion, but the central thrust of the book is an exploration of the increasing "paramilitarization" of the police, Immigration and Naturalization Service, FBI, and other law enforcement organizations that has led to a wholesale loss of civil rights for minorities.

POPPENDIECK, JANET. *Sweet Charity? Emergency Food and the End of Entitlement.* Penguin Books, New York, 1999. Technically, this is just a study of the emergence of soup kitchens, food pantries, and food banks over the past twenty years. But in analyzing the phenomenon, Poppendieck explores more thoroughly than any other author the contradictions between charity and justice. Does charity impede justice? Do works of charity lessen the pressure on a system to create structures of justice? Does all the energy spent on charity exhaust those who might otherwise work to create new structures?

SCHORR, LIZBETH. *Within Our Reach.* Anchor Books, New York, 1988. Schorr is the traditional "liberal" (not a bad thing to be, in my opinion) who has had a great deal of governmental experience with poverty programs. In the process, she has learned a great deal about programs that function well and have positive results. She focuses on supposedly intractable aspects of poverty and how each of three programs has responded to it. One gets a surprisingly hopeful picture of what has been done and, more important, could be done if we were willing to invest in the process.

SHORRIS, EARL. *New American Blues: A Journey through Poverty to Democracy.* W. W. Norton & Co, New York, 1997. A fascinating and provocative book. Shorris interviewed literally thousands of poor people across the country over the span of a decade. Here he vividly records many of those conversations and intersperses them with his interpretations. His idea that poor people exist within a "surround of force" is as good an analysis of modern oppression as you'll find. Shorris also began a small academy in New York, teaching a traditional classical education at a college level to ghetto residents, and he offers it as a particular approach for solving the problems of poverty for some individuals.

SIDEL, RUTH. *Women and Children Last: The Plight of Poor Women in Affluent America.* Penguin USA, New York, 1992, and

Keeping Women and Children Last: America's War on the Poor.
Penguin USA, New York, 1998. The feminization of poverty in
the United States and the ways in which the status of women has
affected poverty in the country. The second book is not just an
updated reprint but a new book entirely.

SIMON, DAVID AND BURNS, EDWARD. *The Corner: A Year in the
Life of an Inner-City Neighborhood.* Broadway Books, New York,
1998. A chronicle of the life on a few blocks in the inner city of
Baltimore over a twelve-month period during 1993. It is essentially a story of how drug addiction dominates lives and how an
open-air drug market dominates a particular Baltimore neighborhood. The writers spent a year and one half in the neighborhood, apparently earned the trust of the residents, and tell an
amazing story. Although a work of journalism, it reads like a
novel. It's a chilling look at life in the depths of the ghetto.

SKLAR, HOLLY; MYKYTA, LARYSSA; AND WEFALD, SUSAN. *Raise the
Floor: Wages and Policies that Work for All of Us.* Ms. Foundation
for Women, New York, 2001. A cogent and well-reasoned argument for raising the minimum wage to $8.00 an hour, (approxi-
mately what it was in constant dollars in 1968), supported by a
treasure trove of statistics and argument. The authors develop a
"minimum needs budget" (as opposed to the usually used but
inadequate "poverty level") that would mandate, among other
things, an increased minimum wage indexed to inflation.

WEIL, ALAN AND FINEGOLD, KENNETH, eds. *Welfare Reform: The
Next Act.* The Urban Institute Press, Washington, D.C., 2002. In
preparation for the debates reauthorizing the Personal

Responsibility and Work Opportunity Reconciliation Act of 1996 (Welfare Reform), the Urban Institute has summarized its data on the effects of Welfare Reform so far. Since 1996 the Urban Institute, a nonpartisan research and policy think tank, has sponsored the Assessing the New Federalism project, gathering and analyzing data on state policy choices and its effects on low-income people. In addition to reviewing these studies, they make specific policy recommendations for the reauthorization debate.

WILSON, WILLIAM JULIUS: Wilson is an eminent sociologist currently teaching and doing research at Harvard. His books were the first by a liberal to take an honest look at the sorts of "ghetto-related behaviors" that result from the oppression of the inner city.

The Truly Disadvantaged: The Inner City, the Underclass, and Public Policy. University of Chicago Press, Chicago, 1990. Its primary thesis is that the rising rate of single mothers in the ghettos is due to the declining numbers of males who can find jobs to support families, but this is also a good general look at urban poverty from a sociological point of view. Lots of statistics.

When Work Disappears: The World of the New Urban Poor. Vintage Books, New York, 1997. This is a clear and compelling, if academic, picture of poverty in the inner city of Chicago. Wilson's books are a little difficult to read, but his theoretical grasp of the subject is superb and his statistics impressive. He is especially clear about the relationship between declining job prospects and the rise of ghetto-related behaviors.

In addition to the books mentioned above, there are several Web sites that have an impressive range of up-to-date information about American poverty. All allow unlimited downloading *gratis*. Some of the ones I relied upon most heavily are:

THE CENSUS BUREAU. www.census.gov/hhes/www/poverty.html. The government census bureau, of course, has the most complete demographic statistics available, but I have been surprised at how available and well formatted the information is. The Web site is easy to navigate, and I have had little trouble finding the information I wanted. By the time this book is printed, the analysis of the 2000 census should be complete.

THE CENTER FOR BUDGET AND POLICY PRIORITIES. www.cbpp.org. CBPP is an amazingly prolific organization dedicated to writing policy papers on aspects of federal and state budgetary policy that impinge upon social welfare. They are a nonpartisan organization that provides extensive and up-to-date data and analysis.

THE CHILDREN'S DEFENSE FUND. www.childrensdefensefund.org. Marian Wright Edelman's Children's Defense Fund has had a single-minded focus on the well-being of American children, especially poor children, for more than twenty-five years. It is an activist organization that provides excellent analysis along with many ways to get involved in advocacy for children.

THE FEDERAL BUREAU OF JUSTICE. www.ojp.usdoj.gov/bjs/welcome.html. The Bureau of Justice has data on incarceration and sentencing, both federally and state-by-state.

THE INSTITUTE FOR RESEARCH ON POVERTY. www.ssc.wisc.edu/
irp/. A site at the University of Wisconsin that has some basic information on poverty statistics and also sponsors its own research.

THE JOINT CENTER FOR POVERTY RESEARCH. www.jcpr.org.
Funded by the United States Department of Health and Human
Services. In addition to its own information, it has a page of
extensive links, www.jcpr.org/links.html, to many other helpful
Web sites.

THE SENTENCING PROJECT. www.sentencingproject.org. The
Sentencing Project is an advocacy organization working against
the huge increase in incarceration rates over the last twenty
years. In addition to statistics, they have good analysis.

Notes

INTRODUCTION

1. Statistics in this paragraph and the next calculated by the author from Joseph Dalaker, *Poverty in the United States: 2000*, U.S. Census Bureau, Current Population Reports, Series P60-214 (Washington, D.C.: U.S. Government Printing Office, 2001). This table can also be found at www.census.gov/prod/2001pubs/p60-214.pdf.

2. In *New American Blues*, an impressionistic study of the many faces of American poverty, writer and philosopher Earl Shorris describes what he calls the "surround of force" confronting poor people.

3. Eric Lotke, *Hobbling a Generation: Young African-American Men in D.C.'s Criminal Justice System Five Years Later*, a report from the National Center on Institutions and Alternatives, August 1997. This report can be found at www.igc.org/ncia/hobb.html. Cited in Cheryl Thompson, "Washington, D.C., Young Blacks Entangled in Legal System," *Washington Post*, August 26, 1997, p. B1.

4. Conservative social scientist Charles Murray's arguments in *The Bell Curve*—that economic success is largely due to IQ, that the IQ of African Americans averages fifteen points less than Caucasians, and that education has little effect on either—are a recent example. But response to Murray's work from the scientific community was overwhelmingly critical. Science provides no support for the notion of black genetic inferiority.

5. The annotated bibliography on page 133 provides brief descriptions of some of the most important sources in this literature.

6. Dalaker, *Poverty in the United States: 2000*, Table A-2. This table can also be found at www.census.gov/prod/2001pubs/p60-214.pdf.

7. Ibid.

CHAPTER ONE

1. In 1910, the average African-American resident in northern cities lived in a ward that was less than 10 percent black. There has been no comparable

study of southern cities, but "there is little evidence of a distinctive black ghetto in southern cities in the nineteenth century," either. See Douglas Massey and Nancy Denton in *American Apartheid* (Cambridge: Harvard University Press, 1994), pp. 24–25.

2. The word *ghetto* means different things to different people. Sociologists Douglas Massey and Nancy Denton, in their definitive study of American segregation, *American Apartheid*, define the term as "a set of neighborhoods that are exclusively inhabited by members of one group, and within which virtually all members of that group live." (pp. 18–19) By this definition, none of these nineteenth- and early twentieth-century immigrant communities (including the African-American communities) were remotely close to being ghettos. In fact, "by this definition, no ethnic or racial group in the history of the United States, except one [African Americans] has ever experienced ghettoization, even briefly." (p. 19)

3. Joe William Trotter, *Blacks in the Urban North: The "Underclass Question" in Historical Perspective* in *The Underclass Debate*, edited by Michael B. Katz (Princeton: Princeton University Press, 1993), p. 60.

4. Arnold Hirsch, *Making the Second Ghetto* (Chicago: University of Chicago Press, 1983), p. 120.

5. Michael Katz, *The Price of Citizenship* (New York: Metropolitan Books, 2001), p. 40.

6. The black exodus rarely led to real residential integration, however, since whites generally chose to leave the newly integrated areas, creating new, affluent black suburban ghettos.

7. Maurice Isserman and Michael Kazin, *America Divided* (New York: Oxford University Press, 2000), p. 199.

8. Ibid., p. 111.

CHAPTER TWO

1. William Julius Wilson's *The Urban Poverty and Family Life Study* is summarized in his book *When Work Disappears* (New York: Alfred A. Knopf, 1997).

2. "Inner-city black job seekers with limited work experience and little familiarity with the white, middle-class world are also likely to have difficulty in the typical job interview. A spotty work record will have to be justified; misunderstanding and suspicion may undermine rapport and hamper communication. However qualified they are for the job, inner-city black applicants are more likely to fail subjective 'tests' of [future] productivity during the interview." *When Work Disappears*, pp. 132–33.

3. Reported in Massey and Denton, *American Apartheid*, p. 95.

4. Ibid., p. 9. Massey and Denton also write: "The effect of segregation on black well-being is structural, not individual. Residential segregation lies beyond the ability of any individual to change; it constrains black life chances irrespective of personal traits, individual motivations, or private achievements." pp. 2–3.

5. Ibid. "The highest isolation index ever recorded for any ethnic group in any American city was 56 percent (for Milwaukee's Italians in 1910), but by 1970 the *lowest* level of spatial isolation observed for blacks anywhere, north or south, was 56 percent (in San Francisco)." p. 49.

6. Ibid. "Unlike black ghettos, immigrant enclaves were never homogeneous, and always contained a wide variety of nationalities, even if they were publicly associated with a particular national origin group.... A second crucial distinction is that most European ethnics [of a given city] did not live in immigrant 'ghettos,' as ethnically diluted as they were." p. 32.

7. Andrew Hacker, *Two Nations: Black and White, Separate, Hostile, Unequal* (New York: Ballantine Books, 1995), p. 41.

8. Massey and Denton, *American Apartheid*, p. 91. Massey and Denton quote studies showing that by "large majorities, blacks support the ideal of integration and express a preference for integrated living, and 95 percent are willing to live in neighborhoods that are anywhere between 15 percent and 70 percent black."

9. To simplify, assume a small community of 1,000 people—900 whites and 100 blacks. Assume further that 90 of the whites and 20 of the blacks are poor—an average rate of poverty of 11 percent (110 of 1,000). If black and white, rich and poor were evenly distributed ("perfect integration"), therefore, everyone would live in a neighborhood that has a poverty rate of 11 percent. If African Americans become completely segregated, however, their segregated neighborhood in the community now has a poverty rate of 20 out of 100, or 20 percent. Whites, on the other hand, now live in neighborhoods with a poverty rate of 90 out of 900, or 10 percent. Segregation has *concentrated* an average community poverty rate that was 11 percent so that all black people now live in a neighborhood with a 20-percent poverty rate. The following table gives the same data:

	No. of people	No. of poor	Poverty rate
Under integrated conditions			
Entire community	1,000	110	11%
Under segregated conditions			
White neighborhood	900	90	10%
Black neighborhood	100	20	20%

10. Massey and Denton, *American Apartheid*: "To the extent that property own-
    ers perceive a decline as possible or likely, they have little incentive to invest
    in upkeep and improvements on their own buildings, because money put into
    neighborhoods that are declining is unlikely to be recouped in the form of high
    rents or greater home equity....At some point a threshold is crossed beyond
    which the pattern becomes self-reinforcing and irreversible." pp. 131–32.

11. In *Savage Inequalities* (New York: Crown Publishers, 1991) educator
    Jonathan Kozol graphically describes his visits to schools in poor areas across
    the country and his discussions with teachers and students. In an East St.
    Louis junior high school, Kozol asks about Martin Luther King, Jr., and a
    young student, Christopher, remarks,

    > "Don't tell students in this school about 'the dream.' Go and
    > look into a toilet here if you would like to know what life is like
    > for students in this city."
    >   Before I leave, I do as Christopher asked and enter a boys'
    > bathroom. Four of the six toilets do not work. The toilet stalls,
    > which are eaten away by red and brown corrosion, have no doors.
    > The toilets have no seats. One has a rotted wooden stump. There
    > are no paper towels and no soap. Near the door there is a loop of
    > wire with an empty toilet-paper roll.
    >   "This," says Sister Julia, "is the best school that we have in
    > East St. Louis."...
    >   Almost anyone who visits in the schools of East St. Louis,
    > even for a short time, comes away profoundly shaken. These are
    > innocent children, after all. They have done nothing wrong.
    > They have committed no crime. They are too young to have
    > offended us in any way at all. One searches for some way to
    > understand why a society as rich and, frequently, as generous as
    > ours would leave these children in their penury and squalor for
    > so long—and with so little public indignation. Is this just a
    > strange mistake of history? (pp. 36, 40)

    It is no mistake. In such schools, when compared to their non-ghetto coun-
    terparts, the physical condition of the buildings, the paucity of equipment
    and supplies, the quality of instruction, the size of classes, and what is
    expected of the students, like almost everything else about such schools, cry
    out for justice.

12. Jay Greene, *High School Graduation Rates in the United States* (New York:
    Manhattan Institute for Policy Research, 2001), Table 8. This study is also
    available at www.schoolchoiceinfo.org/hot_topics/pdf/67.pdf.

13. Robert Mills, *Health Insurance Coverage: 2000*, U.S. Census Bureau, Current
    Population Reports (Washington, D.C.: U.S. Government Printing Office,

2001). This report can also be found at www.census.gov/hhes/www/ hlthins.html.

14. The Centers for Disease Control and Prevention, "Poverty and Infant Mortality—United States, 1988," published in *Morbidity and Mortality Weekly Report (MMWR)* 44 (1995):922–27. Cited in Dennis Andrulis, *The Urban Health Penalty: New Dimensions and Directions in Inner-City Health Care* (American College of Physicians: American Society of Internal Medicine, Division of Governmental Affairs and Public Policy, 2011 Pennsylvania Avenue NW, Suite 800, Washington, D.C. 10006). This review of the literature, with its citations, can be found at www.acponline.org/ hpp/pospaper/andrulis.htm.

15. S. Oakie, "Study Links Cancer, Poverty: Blacks' Higher Rates are Tied to Income," *Washington Post*, April 17, 1991. This study, based on a National Cancer Institute study in three major cities, indicated that poverty had a much greater influence on cancer rates than did race or culture. Cited in Andrulis, *The Urban Health Penalty*.

16. O. Fein, "The Influence of Social Class on Health Status: American and British Research on Health Inequalities," *Journal of General Internal Medicine* 10(1995): 577–86. Cited in Andrulis, *The Urban Health Penalty*.

17. R. G. Wilkinson, "Income Distribution and Life Expectancy," *British Medical Journal* 304(1992): 165–68.

18. George Kaplan et al., "Inequality in Income and Mortality in the United States," *British Medical Journal* 312(1996): 999–1000.

19. World Health Organization (WHO), *World Health Report 2000*, Annex Table 2. This report can be found at www.who.int/whr/2000.

20. *The Nature and Extent of Lead Poisoning in Children in the United States: A Report to Congress* (Washington, D.C.: Agency for Toxic Substances and Disease Registry, 1988). Cited in Andrulis, *The Urban Health Penalty*.

21. "The State of America's Children," *Children's Defense Fund Yearbook 2001* (Washington, D.C., 2001), p. 39.

22. D. M. Mannino; D. M. Homa; C. A. Pertowski et al., "Surveillance for asthma—United States, 1960–1995," *Morbidity and Mortality Weekly Report (MMWR)/CDC Surveillance Summaries* 47(1998):1–27.

23. Mark Nord et al., *Household Food Security in the United States, 2000*, p. 4. This report can be found at www.ers.usda.gov/publications/fanrr21.

24. Ibid., p. 11.

25. Elliott Currie, *Crime and Punishment in America* (New York: Henry Holt and Company, 1998), p. 49.

26. "Facts about Prisons and Prisoners," The Sentencing Project, 2002. The Sentencing Project is located at 514 Tenth Street NW, Suite 1000, Washington, D.C. 20004. A copy of this document can be found at www.sentencingproject.org/brief/pub1035.pdf.

27. *Sourcebook of Criminal Justice Statistics 2000*, 28th edition (Bureau of Justice Statistics), Table 6.1. The Sourcebook can be found at www.albany.edu/sourcebook.

28. International comparisons taken from The Sentencing Project tables found at www.sentencingproject.org/news/usno1.pdf.

29. Currie, *Crime and Punishment in America*, p. 13.

30. Lotke, *Hobbling a Generation*.

31. Currie, *Crime and Punishment in America*, p. 13.

32. Glenda Cooper, "Drug Cases, Sentences Up Sharply Since 1984," *Washington Post*, August 20, 2001.

33. Currie, *Crime and Punishment in America*, p. 77.

34. William Finnegan, *Cold New World* (New York: Random House, 1999), p. xx.

35. Jonathan P. Caulkins et al., *Mandatory Minimum Drug Sentences: Throwing Away the Key or the Taxpayers' Money?* (Santa Monica, Calif.: RAND, 1997), pp. xvii–xviii.

36. *Sourcebook of Criminal Justice Statistics 2000*, Table 1-1.

37. U.S. Census: Historical CPS Income Tables: Median Income by Educational Attainment, Tables P-16 and P-17. These tables can be found at www.census.gov/income/ftp/histinc/people/p16.lst and www.census.gov/income/ftp/histinc/people/p17.lst.

38. Ibid.

CHAPTER THREE

1. William Julius Wilson, *When Work Disappears* (New York: Alfred A. Knopf, 1997), p. 55. On the choice to engage in ghetto-related behaviors, Wilson writes, "This is not to argue that individuals and groups lack the freedom to make their own choices, engage in certain conduct, and develop certain styles and orientations, but it is to say that these decisions and actions occur with-

in a context of constraints and opportunities that are drastically different from those present in middle-class society."

2. Ibid., p. 92.

3. Ibid.

4. Ibid., p. 89.

5. Rebecca Blank, *It Takes a Nation* (Princeton, N.J.: Princeton University Press, 1997), p. 33.

6. Wilson, *When Work Disappears*, pp. 87–88.

7. "The State of America's Children," p. 50.

8. Gina Adams and Monica Rohacek, "Child Care and Welfare Reform," in *Welfare Reform: The Next Act*, edited by Alan Weil and Kenneth Finegold (Washington, D.C.: The Urban Institute Press, 2002), p. 122.

9. Ibid., p 46.

10. Blank, *It Takes a Nation*, p. 44.

11. Ibid.

12. Some states and the District of Columbia are experimenting with "earned income disregards," allowing single mothers to keep more of such extra income.

13. Blank, *It Takes a Nation*, p. 45.

14. William Julius Wilson explores this phenomenon, which he calls the "male marriageable-pool index," in *The Truly Disadvantaged* (Chicago: The University of Chicago Press, 1987). See especially pp. 83–106.

15. Blank, *It Takes a Nation*, p. 40.

16. Since no baby should be labeled *illegitimate*, the term's virtual disappearance from our language should be considered progress.

17. *Health, United States, 2001* (Hyattsville, Md.: National Center for Health Statistics, 2001), Table 9, p. 139. This table can be found at www.cdc.gov/nchs/products/pubs/pubd/hus/tables/2001/01hus009.pdf.

18. Rate calculated by author from data in Census Bureau report *Educational Attainment in the United States, March 2000*, Table 5a, available at www.census.gov/population/socdemo/education/p20-536/tab05a.txt.

19. Ibid.

20. Geoffrey Canada, *Fist, Stick, Knife, Gun: A Personal History of Violence in America* (Boston: Beacon Press, 1995).

21. Currie, *Crime and Punishment in America*, p. 58.

22. "HIV/AIDS Among African Americans," Centers for Disease Control and Prevention, Division of HIV/AIDS Prevention. This fact sheet can be found at www.cdc.gov/hiv/pubs/facts/afam.htm.

23. For example, the Centers for Disease Control and Prevention's 1998 edition of its publication, *Trends in the HIV/AIDS Epidemic*, points out that "[t]he data suggest that three interrelated issues play a role [in the epidemic]—the continued health disparities between economic classes, our nation's inability to successfully deal with substance abuse, and the intersection between substance abuse and the epidemic of HIV and other sexually transmitted diseases." p. 8.

24. When groups of people—especially children—mix freely, differences in accent and dialect diminish. Black English Vernacular differs substantially from Standard English, indicating a high degree of segregation and isolation.

25. Massey and Denton, *American Apartheid*, p. 168.

CHAPTER FOUR

1. Historian Michael B. Katz writes, "Welfare has also been deployed to regulate labor markets by manipulating work incentives. In practice, this has meant goading working-class men and women to labor hard for low wages by frightening them with the prospect of a subhuman and stigmatized descent into the ranks of paupers." *In the Shadow of the Poorhouse* (New York: Basic Books, 1996), p. xi.

2. Gretchen Rowe, "State TANF Policies as of 1999," Table II.A.3 (Washington, D.C.: The Urban Institute, 2000), p. 74. Also available at newfederalism.urban.org/pdf/Wrd.pdf.

3. Katz, *In the Shadow of the Poorhouse*: "The resilient distinction between social insurance and public assistance reflects the long-standing suspicion of...welfare. There remains...a lurking assumption that many of those who ask for help neither need nor deserve it. By contrast, social insurance is acceptable because, so it is believed, it is earned. With their own wages, workers contribute to funds—supplemented by their employers—that will support them in periods of unemployment or in old age. Even though they may take out far more than they contribute, they can argue that they have paid their way. Equally important, social insurance is popular because its benefits cross class lines. Almost everybody is eligible for social security retirement benefits." p. 246

4. Ibid. The "bifurcation of welfare into social insurance and public assistance trapped the architects of...Johnson's Great Society who wanted to wage war on

poverty. For it ruled out any serious attempt to redistribute wealth, guarantee incomes, or tamper with the structure of American capitalism.... Unwilling to explain poverty as an inescapable consequence of American political economy, they had two alternatives. One was to place the blame squarely on individuals and to redefine poverty as evidence of moral or intellectual incompetence. The other was to see it as the result of artificial and unjustifiable barriers...inimical to the open and competitive structure of American life. In practice, explanations drifted between both poles." pp. 259, 263.

5. U.S. Census Bureau, Historical Poverty Tables, Table 2, available at www.census.gov/hhes/poverty/histpov/hstpov2.html.

6. Although partially federally funded, Medicaid is a locally administered program. Not enough funds have been appropriated to cover all who are poor, so each state decides how to allocate those funds. The District of Columbia, for example, gives benefits only to those poor who are completely disabled or the parents of small children.

7. Crime rates are higher among late adolescents and early adults, so the Baby Boomer bulge would normally have led to higher crime rates.

8. Wilson, *When Work Disappears*, p. 49.

9. In one notorious example, the Administration actually tried to declare ketchup a vegetable so that program requirements for a certain number of vegetable servings in the diets of school children could be partially met by the ketchup provided. Fortunately, public reaction short-circuited the attempt.

10. Cushing Dolbeare, *Changing Priorities: The Federal Budget and Housing Assistance, 1976–2006* (Washington, D.C.: National Low-Income Housing Coalition, 2001), Table 4. This table is available at www.nlihc.org/pubs/appendixbtable4.htm.

11. Kathryn Edin and Laura Lein, *Making Ends Meet* (New York: Russell Sage Foundation, 1997).

12. Barbara Vobejda and Judith Havemann, "Welfare Clients Already Work Off the Books," *Washington Post*, November 3, 1997.

13. AFDC, of course, was not available to adults without children, and most states had, by this time, eliminated general assistance to these people, too.

14. Social Security Administration, *Welfare Reform SSI Childhood Disability Factsheet 1997*.

15. Tommy Thompson, "A Considered Opinion: Welfare's Next Step," in *The Brookings Report on Welfare* 19:3(Summer 2001): 2.

16. *Wisconsin Works (W-2) Program*, Wisconsin Legislative Audit Bureau Audit Summary, April 2001, available at www.legis.state.wi.us/lab/Reports/01-7tear.htm.

17. Zoë Neuberger, *States are Already Cutting Child Care and TANF–Funded Programs*, Center for Budget and Policy Priorities, May 16, 2002. This report can be found at www.cbpp.org/5-16-02wel.htm.

18. Urban Institute, Single-Parent Earnings Monitor, July 2001, available at www.urban.org/pdfs/SPEM_1.pdf.

19. Pamela Loprest, "Making the Transition from Welfare to Work," in *Welfare Reform: The Next Act*, edited by Alan Weil and Kenneth Finegold (Washington, D.C.: The Urban Institute Press, 2002), p. 20.

20. Dan Bloom and Don Winstead, *Sanctions and Welfare Reform*, Brookings Policy Brief #12, January 2002, p. 3, available at www.brookings.edu/wrb/publications/pb/pb12.pdf.

21. Pamela Loprest and Sheila Zedlewski, "Current and Former Welfare Recipients: How Do They Differ?," Discussion Paper 99-17 (Washington, D.C.: The Urban Institute, 1999), Table 2.

22. Andres Cherlin et al., "Welfare, Children, and Families: A Three-City Study," in *Johns Hopkins University Policy Brief* 01-1, p. 5.

23. Jocelyn Guyer et al., "Millions of Mothers Lack Health Insurance Coverage," Center for Budget and Policy Priorities, Washington, D.C.: 2001, available at www.cbpp.org/5-10-01health.pdf.

24. Sheila Zedlewski and Amelia Gruber, "Former Welfare Families and the Food Stamp Program: The Exodus Continues," Urban Institute Policy Paper B-33 (Washington, D.C.: The Urban Institute, 2001), Figure 2. This article is available at www.urban.org.

25. Jocelyn Guyer, "Health Care after Welfare: An Update of Findings from State-Level Leaver Studies," Center for Budget and Policy Priorities, Washington, D.C.: 2000, available at www.cbpp.org/8-16-00wel.htm.

26. "The State of America's Children," p. 46.

27. Adams and Rohacek, "Child Care and Welfare Reform," in *Welfare Reform*, edited by Weil and Finegold, p 122.

28. Adams and Rohacek, "Child Care and Welfare Reform," in *Welfare Reform*, edited by Weil and Finegold, p. xxi.

29. While the actual formula is very complex, the basic process is that Social Security produces an average, indexed (adjusting for inflation over the lifetime of the recipient) monthly income over thirty-five years of work.

Currently, a retiree will receive as his or her Social Security benefit 90 percent of the first $561 of that average, indexed, monthly income, 32 percent of the amount between $561 and $3,381, and 15 percent of the amount more than $3,381.

CHAPTER FIVE

1. All dollar amounts are approximations based on actual figures in Finnish marks; they fluctuate, of course, according to the exchange rate.

2. A single mother with one child would, therefore, receive $265 a month for that child ($100 basic payment, $125 from the child's father, and $40 single-parent compensation. For two children, she would be paid $535 a month in family support payments alone.

3. A single mother with one child under the age of three and another between three and seven would, therefore, receive $660 a month for staying home and taking care of the children. Adding family support to home–child care support, she would receive government support of $1,220 a month.

4. Finland follows the international standard for computing the poverty line at half the median income. United States poverty levels would generally be higher if we used this standard.

5. Buying work tools, additional childcare needs, moving expenses, or funeral expenses are examples of special needs.

6. If an unemployed person refuses an appropriate job offer, for example, this support can be reduced by 20 percent for several months. If that person refuses another job in the same time period, the support can be reduced 40 percent. The reductions last only several months, however, at which point the person is given another chance.

CHAPTER SIX

1. David Himmelstein and Steffie Woolhandler, *The National Health Program Chartbook*, Physicians for a National Health Program, Chicago, 1992, p. 145. In each of nine local and national polls, more than 60 percent favored tax-financed health insurance. See *USA Today*/Harris Poll, *USA Today*, November 23, 1998, and Al Hunt, "NBC/*Wall Street Journal* Poll," *Wall Street Journal*, June 25, 1998.

2. Physicians for a National Health Program has proposed a plan very similar to McDermott's bill. The details of such a plan can be obtained from PNHP

at 332 South Michigan, Suite 500, Chicago, IL 60604, or from their Web site at www.pnhp.org.

3. When large corporations decide for their own reasons (such as corporate mergers) to lay off tens of thousands of workers, those lost jobs are considered an unfortunate but necessary price of higher efficiency in business, and few within the corporate world argue against the logic of the lost jobs. That is the way, we are told, the economy evolves to become stronger. A much better case can be made that the evolution to universal health insurance would strengthen our nation considerably.

4. Since President Bill Clinton's unsuccessful attempt to reform health care at the beginning of his first term (which because of intense political opposition did not include a single-payer plan among the alternatives), the issue has gradually disappeared from the political radar screen.

5. Al Hunt, "NBC/*Wall Street Journal* Poll," *Wall Street Journal*, June 25, 1998.

6. According to Ida Hellender at Physicians for a National Health Program, these are the most recent general polls.

7. *Poverty Rate Hits Lowest Level Since 1979 as Unemployment Reaches a 30-Year Low*, Center for Budget and Policy Priorities, Washington, D.C., 2000, available at www.cbpp.org/9-26-00pov.htm.

8. Cushing Dolbeare, *Changing Priorities: The Federal Budget and Housing Assistance, 1976–2006* (Washington, D.C.: National Low-Income Housing Coalition, 2001), p. 9, available at www.nlihc.org/pubs/changingpriorities.pdf.

9. Robert Greenstein and Isaac Shapiro, *New Research Findings on the Effects of the Earned Income Tax Credit*, a Center on Budget and Policy Priorities study: "A series of studies…[has] consistently found that the EITC has substantial positive effects in inducing single parents to go to work. One of the most important of these studies finds that the proportion of single mothers who are in the labor force rose sharply between 1984 and 1996 and that the EITC expansions instituted during this period are responsible for more than half of this increase." The Center on Budget and Policy Priorities is located at 820 First St. NE, Suite 510, Washington, D.C. 20002. Its Web site is www.cbpp.org, from which the entire report (along with *much* other useful information) can be downloaded.